Erik

LOVE

AT FIRST

SITE

TIPS AND TALES FOR
ONLINE DATING SUCCESS
FROM A MODERN-DAY MATCHMAKER

RIVER GROVE
BOOKS

Published by River Grove Books
Austin, TX
www.rivergrovebooks.com

Distributed by River Grove Books

For ordering information or special discounts for bulk purchases,
please contact River Grove Books at PO Box 91869, Austin, TX
78709, 512.891.6100.

Design and composition by Greenleaf Book Group
Cover design by Greenleaf Book Group
Cover photo by Joe LeBlanc

Publisher's Cataloging-In-Publication Data
Ettin, Erika.
   Love at first site : tips and tales for online dating success from a
modern-day matchmaker / Erika Ettin.—First edition.
     pages : illustrations ; cm
   Issued also as an ebook.
   ISBN: 978-1-63299-013-6
   1. Online dating—Handbooks, manuals, etc. 2. Dating (Social
customs)—Case studies. 3. Interpersonal relations. 4. Courtship.
I. Title.
HQ801.82 .E88 2014
306.730285   2014939304

eBook ISBN: 978-1-63299-014-3

First Edition

For anyone who has ever followed a passion, leaving the beaten path and instead pursuing the road less traveled. And, of course, for all of the amazing single men and women out there who might need "a little nudge" to go after what they want.

TABLE OF CONTENTS

Section 5: Searching and Emailing

Section 6: Safety First

Section 7: The First Date

Section 8: The Follow-up

ACKNOWLEDGMENTS

My journey as an entrepreneur has not been a straight path, but rather a winding road that took me through an economics degree in college, a seven-and-a-half-year career in finance, and an MBA at night. All of this happened before I realized my true calling—writing and helping people with online dating. I learned that it's more important to take a risk and follow your dreams than to have a comfortable, yet not exciting, career . . . even if you end up working three times the number of hours you did before!

Thank you to my family and my friends for your continued support and encouragement. I would not be who I am today without your support. I want to specifically thank my mom Joyce and my sister Elyse, who painstakingly read each and every one of my articles before they were published. I would also like to thank my friend Betsy, who is the best cheerleader a gal could ask for. In addition, I want to thank the team at Sixth & I for inadvertently coming up with my book title. I love you all!

INTRODUCTION

You may be wondering how I got into the crazy field of online dating consulting. Good question. It's not like Cornell offered a class called "Online Dating 101" when I was there. (I bet that would have been a fun class, though!) I was actually an early adopter of online dating, starting to use JDate (a site to meet a Jewish partner) in 2001, which was well before people really had any idea what it was all about. My parents, naturally, flipped out, thinking I was going to meet some psycho-killer, or worse, someone who wasn't worthy of their daughter! The worst that happened, of course, was a few bad dates with some socially awkward men . . . er . . . boys who were clueless as to what dating actually entailed. But why not try? I was technologically savvy. I mean, I did have a cell phone in college before anyone else did, even if it was this giant blue boxy thing that I didn't want anyone to know I had. (It was very *uncool* to have a cell phone back then. My, how times have changed!)

I had some relationships throughout college and afterwards, some with people I met while online dating and others I met in "real life." Between every relationship, though, I logged back onto JDate, thinking, "What if?" In 2009, I made a major push to meet the man of my dreams. And as someone who gets really focused on a project (in other words, I'm fairly Type A), I rarely do anything halfway. I was often going on four, five, or six dates a week (no shame in booking two back-to-back dates in one evening). At that point, my friends were taking notice. I was getting questions from them like, "What are you doing that I'm not?" and "Will you read my profile to see if it's any good?" Someone I had once gone out with for about two months even asked me to look at his profile. At that point, I knew I had something going for me. So, I proceeded to write and rewrite friends' profiles, and lo and behold, they did better, getting more attention online and going on more dates.

On the other side of my life, I was working at Fannie Mae. (I think my last job title there was Senior Financial Economist. Not too shabby, right?) While it was a great job and the work was somewhat interesting—though not really to me—I knew I couldn't spend the rest of my life behind a desk or in a cubicle. In fact, my former boss tried to urge me to find a more fulfilling career long before I decided that for myself. With some deep thought and some urging from my boyfriend at the time (yes, from JDate), I took a leap of faith and quit my job at Fannie Mae to move on to greener pastures. In my case, these greener pastures were in the form of starting my own business, A Little Nudge.

Ironically enough, even though I had my MBA, I felt like I didn't know the first thing about actually starting a business. Yes, I did know how to write an excellent business plan, and since my background is in economics, I knew that keeping the finances for the business wouldn't be a problem. I didn't know the basic things, though, like taking credit card payments (the iPhone/iPad plug-ins like Square didn't yet exist) or building a website. So I did a lot of reading, got my ducks in a row, and declared that my last day at Fannie Mae would be March 25, 2011. That was one of the best decisions I've ever made.

I started with some "beta" clients—a friend, a former coworker (who volunteered himself when I sent my "I'm leaving" email to my team at Fannie Mae), and a friend's cousin—all three of whom are now happily married. (Insert pat on the back here.) Then I was open for business. Since then, I have worked with hundreds of clients all around the United States and other countries, including Israel, Australia, and the UK. I help people with all aspects of online dating, from writing a profile to catch someone's attention to sending emails that get noticed to planning dates.

I have never been as happy as I am doing the work I'm doing, both as an entrepreneur and as a dating coach. Seeing my clients, many of whom are now married or engaged, in happy relationships or simply getting them out there again fills my life with such a sense of pride.

I'm hoping that, with this book, you not only learn how to online date effectively, but you also get to share in the joy that I get from helping people. As you'll see, this book is mainly geared towards opposite-sex couples, but all of the same concepts apply for same-sex couples as well.

Section 1

PROFILE PICTURES

In this section, you'll learn:

- Which online dating photos work and which don't
- How many photos to use in your profile
- Why the photos are so darn important anyway
- Whether or not taking professional photos is a good idea

Chapter 1

THE FIVE RULES OF THUMB

Anyone who has ever used an online dating site will understand when I say that some people's profile pictures are, well, less than flattering. I've seen it all—the shirtless bathroom selfie (often with dirty laundry sitting in the background), the photos of your last ski trip where all I can see is some guy in a ski mask, and the photo of you sleeping.

When it comes to online dating photos, I recommend using only three to five. With this in mind, let's look at the **five rules of thumb** for choosing your online dating photos.

RULE #1: USE A CLEAR "FACE" PHOTO AS YOUR MAIN PROFILE PICTURE

On most online dating sites, you come up as a thumbnail, or a tiny, postage stamp-sized image that allows someone to briefly sneak a peek at you. If your photo is blurry or you're standing too far away from the camera, people can't see what you look like, so they won't even get as far as clicking on your profile.

If you don't have at least one clear head shot as your main profile picture, your profile will scream, "I'm hiding something!"

or worse, "I can't even find a friend to snap a decent picture!" You really don't want someone to pass you over simply because he or she can't see what you look like at first glance.

Some people may not click on her profile simply because this photo is a bit blurry.

This one is clear and just beautiful.

THE MORAL: Blurry photos don't help anyone, and they do hurt you.

RULE #2: LESS IS MORE

Would you believe that Match.com allows a whopping 26 online dating profile photos? (I didn't believe it, either!) When I used JDate in the olden days—before the fairly recent format change—only four pictures were allowed. Now, the site allows 12. I believe JDate's former rule of limiting the number of pictures to four was actually for the better. Let's say I have eight photos of myself on an online dating site. In four of them, I look really cute (two in a hot pink dress and two more in a pair of jeans and my favorite red sweater); in two, I look just okay (bad hair day . . . others with curly hair can relate); and in the remaining two, for one reason or another, I just don't look as good (*really* bad hair day, perhaps). My potential suitor may think that I'm the gal for him based on the first couple of pictures alone, but by the time he gets to the eighth one, he has already dismissed me, thinking that those bad pictures reflect what I actually look like. Clearly they do not, but he doesn't know that.

A picture is worth a thousand words, but 10 pictures are a waste of time. Now that Facebook has taken over the world, when it comes to online dating profiles, people often confuse the concept of posting just a few flattering pictures with posting an entire album. I have no doubt that your pictures from your trip to Greece with you standing on the Acropolis are amazing. Just remember, there's a time and a place for them, and that place is not an online dating site.

With these three pictures alone, this gentleman would do quite well.

© Junial Enterprises, 2014

By adding these two additional pictures—one where he looks like he has a bone to pick with someone and the other just plain ridiculous—anyone who is interested initially may dismiss him, simply because he gave too much information.

THE MORAL: Three great photos win over four or more mediocre photos any day. People will look for the one bad photo and decide not to email you because of it.

RULE #3: BE BY YOURSELF IN THE SHOT

A client recently told me that someone emailed her on Match.com asking if he could have her friend's number. (It's a groaner, I know.) My client was confused for a moment and then realized that he had looked at her pictures, one of which included some girlfriends, and concluded that her friend was the woman of his dreams.

Online dating experts often give conflicting advice: three pictures versus five pictures, a long profile versus a short one, listing your salary range versus leaving it blank. But there's one online dating pointer that most experts can agree on: Be by yourself in your online dating pictures. The last thing you want is to be compared to someone else in your own profile, like my poor client.

People have all kinds of reasons for including others in their photos, and I'm here to debunk all of them and then add two caveats for when it's A-okay to share some screen time with someone else.

I want to show that I'm social.

If you're trying to show that you're social by including a picture of you with your friends, it often does the exact opposite; it looks like you're trying too hard to show that you're social. If you have an active social life, your profile should list some of the activities you like to do (kickball, poker, sailing club, etc.), and you'll therefore have no need to prove it in a picture. We also don't want to make anyone pause to wonder whose profile this is. Remember—don't let people compare you to your friends!

Look at me! I'm social because I go to the beach with my friends. But which one am I again?

I guess I can have fun on my own, too.

I want to show that really attractive people (often of the opposite sex) like me.

The next picture is intimidating on many levels. 1) It makes the people looking at your profile compare themselves to your picture-mates to determine whether they are attractive enough for you. 2) It looks a bit conceited, like you exclusively spend time with only extremely attractive people.

3) It makes the people looking at your profile wonder if all of your friends are of the opposite sex. Is there even room for someone else in your life? Lose-lose-lose.

This picture is intimidating on many levels. I'd be nervous to contact this gentleman since he already has so many attractive women in his life.

While I would not recommend using a photo with sunglasses on as the main profile picture (it's too hard to see someone's eyes), this is a good supplementary picture for this profile. There is no need to show the other people in the photo; he's attractive on his own.

I want to show how attractive my ex was so people can see who's in my league.

This picture is also intimidating. 1) We compare ourselves. 2) We think you're not over the ex if he or she still takes a prominent spot in your profile. 3) If you're in a picture with just one other person of the opposite sex, we assume it's an ex, even if it's just a brother or sister. Again, lose-lose-lose.

I think this gentleman might be a good fit, but I don't want to see him with this cute woman.

It turns out he looks pretty nice on his own . . .
actually, even nicer.

I want to show how good-looking I am compared to the rest of my friends.

This faulty strategy has the opposite effect of the points previously made. People may think that you're only attracted to friends who aren't as attractive as you are and wonder why. (I know it seems silly.) Or, more likely, they'll see right through it. Shallow? Yes. True? Yes. I'll spare you the example for this one.

What are the two caveats? Children and pets. If you have children, then it's completely your choice as to whether or not to include a photo with them. If you do decide to post a picture with your child(ren), then just one is sufficient, and please add a caption saying that these are your children, lest someone assume something else. For pets, again, one picture with Fido is plenty. And please don't just show a picture of your pet without you in it. For all we know, you stopped some guy on the street and asked to take a picture of his pup! You may laugh, but it happens.

THE MORAL: Being alone is best . . . in your online dating profile picture, that is.

RULE #4: HAVE ONE PHOTO WHERE YOU ARE DOING SOMETHING INTERESTING

Many people have no idea what to say in the initial email to show someone that they have an interest in communicating. For this reason, it's best to give these potential suitors (or suitor-esses) one more thing to comment about. In other words, provide them with some "email bait."

In my old JDate profile, I had a photo of myself singing *The Star-Spangled Banner*. I received almost-daily emails asking where I was singing and how I got the gig. (Answers: A Washington Nationals game. A good demo and a lot of persistence.) This picture alone gave men the "in" they needed to strike up a conversation.

Other examples clients have used are:

- A woman playing ice hockey in full gear
- A man dressed as a clown since he performs for children every Sunday
- A woman bouncing on a large "egg" trampoline

- A man holding a ridiculously large pumpkin that looks like it should be featured in the *Guinness Book of World Records*
- A woman posing next to a sign that reads "Completely Nuts" (Oh wait—that was me again!)

I'm going to use myself for this example:

This is a cute picture that was taken of me at a baseball game a few years ago (older than I'd recommend using for the photo, but it will get the point across), but it's not really showing anything unique or special.

This photo instead shows me singing at that same Washington Nationals game. It was one of the best nights of my life, and when I used one of these photos on JDate, I got questions about it almost daily.

THE MORAL: Many people have no idea what to say in the initial email, so give them something easy to comment about, or "email bait."

RULE #5: BE ACCURATE

Have you ever walked into the coffee shop or bar for your first date with someone you corresponded with online, and you can't find the person you're supposed to meet? Is it because your date isn't there? Nope! It's because the person looks nothing like his or her pictures. Perhaps old pictures were posted, or perhaps good old Dr. Photoshop made a cameo. Sadly, this happens a lot.

If you lie in your online dating photos with the hope that you'll get to the date and "wow" the other person with your charm and wit, I have to tell you that this is just not how it works. When your date enters the room, all he or she can think is, "This person has lied to me." Your charm is hidden behind the stinky layer of deceit all over you. So before trying to use your college photo to pass for your 45-year-old self, think again about how your date may react to your fib. Do the right thing and tell the truth.

It's better to have someone meet you in person and think, "He or she is so much more attractive than the photos I saw," instead of thinking, "Wow—those photos were a lie . . . or taken five years ago!" I recommend using photos taken within the last year, or even more recently if you've changed something significant about your appearance, like getting a very noticeable haircut or losing/gaining a significant amount of weight.

© Stocklite, 2014. Used under license from Shutterstock.com

If this is the photo you saw of this woman online . . .

... you wouldn't want to instead meet *this* woman on your date. And that's not because she's unattractive; it's because her photo wasn't accurate. It's actually the same woman, believe it or not, but the haircut is so drastic that it's hard to even recognize her.

THE MORAL: Don't lie about your looks . . . enough said.

This leads me to the biggest photo myth: Professional photos are frowned upon. Not true!

If you are going to take professional photos, just make sure they are in a natural setting versus in a contrived studio. Think trees, park benches, and sidewalks, not backdrops, awkward poses, and saccharine-sweet smiles. If you look good, no one will care who took the pictures or whether you paid for them. They'll just be happy they found someone so attractive!

Try to take shots in two different outfits for some variety. For men, one of the outfits should be something you'd wear out to a nice dinner—perhaps a pair of slacks, a long-sleeved buttoned shirt, and nice shoes. (Make sure the shoes match the belt!) For the other outfit, wear something casual that you think represents you. Perhaps that's a pair of jeans and a polo shirt. For women, following the "dinner outfit" recommendation, a casual dress or a nice pair of slacks and a blouse would work. For the other outfit, again, choose something more casual, like a pair of jeans and a flattering top. V-necks tend to look best on women, and studies have shown that red is the best color to wear. Why red? One particular study has two explanations[1]:

1. Red is associated with love—plain and simple.
2. People flush red when they are sexually receptive, thus associating the color with attraction for the other person.

That's quite the correlation. They say the same is true for both men and women, so start stocking up on red clothes. Before you go on that red-shirt shopping spree, though, remember that simply posting a picture in your brand spankin' new red shirt is not the golden ticket to getting you a date every night of the week. The most important part of the picture is still you, and only you.

Lastly, try to avoid crazy patterns, like Hawaiian prints or huge flowers, since we want the attention to be on your face, not on the leis that are adorning the shirt you bought last year on vacation. Also, try to avoid solid white, as it tends to wash people out in their photos. The thing to keep in mind is that you want the attention on you, not on your clothes, for better or for worse.

Q&A with Erika

Q: Her photo from online was obviously an old photo. Anyway, when we met, I felt a little tricked. Is this something I'm going to run into with online dating?
—Dennis, 40, Austin, TX

A: It's just too bad she used old photos. That's a sign of lack of confidence, as I'm sure you figured out. You had every right to feel tricked. Unfortunately, some people resort to lying, but you can't assume that the majority of people will. Take the picture for what it is without assuming anything. You'll be disappointed by some and pleasantly surprised by others.

GATHER AROUND . . . IT'S STORY TIME!

Déjà Vu

As you already know, I was an early adopter of online dating, starting in college when I was home in New Jersey for the summer. I remember my parents being terrified the first time I mentioned that I was going out with someone I met . . . *dun dun dun* . . . online. "What? Who are you going out with? From a website? Is that safe?" (Years later, by the way, my parents *begged* me to let them pay for a membership to JDate. It's amazing what a few years can do.) Anyway, in that first venture into the murky waters of online dating, I met Gerry. We went out for sushi. (I didn't know at the time that dinner was a terrible idea for a first online date, which I'll get to later.) He seemed nice enough, albeit totally nerdy. Now, I'm a nerd in my own right—I sure do love a good, complicated spreadsheet and a rousing game of Scrabble—but he had a huge cell phone on his belt buckle, and, as I mentioned before, this was well before cell phones were universally used. To this day, by the way, I stand by the opinion that no one should wear one on his or her pants. Ever. That said, the conversation was fine. He ate one sushi roll. What man only eats only one sushi roll!? Now, I know I'm barely pushing three digits on the scale, but I can eat at least two or three rolls! And so, that was the first, and I thought last, date with Gerry.

Fast-forward six years. I lived in the nation's capital, was working at Fannie Mae, and was going to business school at night, so there wasn't much time for going out and meeting new people. Once again, I decided to join JDate for what felt like the 77th time, and I wrote to a guy who seemed like he might be a good fit. He wrote back (yay!), and we started having a really witty conversation. He was intrigued by the fact that I loved musical theater. *Did I even say that in my profile?* He seemed attentive and interested in my being from New Jersey. We shared some puns (I love a good pun!), I swooned, and we decided to meet.

Given my crazy schedule with work and school, the only night I had free was Saturday. Strike one for me. Then, he asked me out for dinner, sushi no less. Strike two for me.

We met at the Metro, and he seemed nice enough, albeit totally nerdy. He had a bomber jacket on that definitely went out of style sometime in the late '80s. But I could look past that. We got to the restaurant, and just as we were about to sit down, he looked at me and said, "I have something I have to tell you." *You just met me—what could you possibly have to tell me?* He continued, "I think we went on a date six years ago." Things went downhill from there. Not only had he recognized me from my pictures, but he also hadn't told me he had recognized me because he knew I didn't like him the first time around and would potentially decline the date! The cell phone had moved from the pants to the jacket, but everything else was the same, down to the sushi. And how did he know I love musical theater? It was because he remembered from the first date that I was in a community theater show (*The Pirates of Penzance*, in case you were curious) with his cousin. He had even emailed this cousin to confirm it was me! This time, you know what I did? I ordered three sushi rolls! That'll (chop) stick it to him! I'm eating all the spicy crunchy tuna I want! By 8:30 p.m., I had had enough. I got in a cab, told the driver the whole ridiculous story, and was in my jammies by 9:00 with a much-needed glass of red wine in hand.

So the next time you're on that bad date, remember that you might be telling the story for years to come. Every bad date is a good story!

THE PROFILE

In this section, you'll learn:

- How to come up with the perfect online dating username
- How to catch someone's attention in the daunting profile box
- Which details to share and which not to share
- How long the profile should be to get the maximum appeal

Many people think that writing an online dating profile is a one-time affair. They try to write it as quickly as humanly possible, getting this seemingly daunting task out of the way in a matter of minutes. They also rarely change it based on its success (or lack thereof). Most people I know spend more time booking a cruise, picking out a new TV, and even deciding what to order on a menu than writing their online dating profile. (I used to keep the most elaborate spreadsheets of my annual cruise options . . . I am a former economist, after all. I probably spent 10 hours doing this silly research below.)

	1	2
Date	Saturday, July 11 or Aug 22	Friday, July 17 or 31
Port(s)	Kings Wharf, Bermuda	Turks & Caicos, Half Moon Kay, Freeport, Bahamas
Nights	5	7
Price (inside)	$649	$899*
Price (outside)	$749	$1019*
Days off work	3.5 to 4	4.5 to 5
Ship	Grandeur of the Seas	Carnival Pride
Pros	I've been on it, and it's nice. Adult pool	Great reviews & new ship, 3 ports, I like Carnival
Cons	Smaller, older ship, small rooms	More expensive and more days off work
Erika's thoughts	Short and sweet, fewest days off work, could be right after graduation	Great dates, but kind of expensive

Note: I did not pick Norwegian with "Freestyle Cruising" because then we have to coordinate everyone having dinner together. I'd rather just be assigned a location and time and show up.

* Says there is a $240 rebate if you book over the phone, but so much easier to just do it online.

The online dating profile, however, is actually one thing that you should really spend your time on. You're putting yourself, not a product or a service, out there for the world to see, so you might as well put your best foot forward!

The next several chapters will take you through the steps to creating that perfect online dating profile so yours doesn't end up like this:

> I love to laugh and have fun. I love to go out on the town sometimes and stay in sometimes. My friends and family are so important to me. I'm looking for someone to grow old with. Looking forward to hearing from you.

Chapter 2

THE USERNAME

What's in a name?

    Henry90210

    283017390

    BlueEyedWriter

    NatsFanFromAK

If I gave you these four online dating usernames (all made up, of course), whose profile do you think you'd click on first? I'd venture to say, solely based on the username, that you'd choose the third or fourth one. Am I right? While the username is sometimes an afterthought for online daters, I encourage you to instead think of it more as an executive summary. It is one additional chance to share an extra tidbit about yourself in online dating land. Using a computer-generated number or your first name is analogous to wearing a black suit and white shirt amidst a line of others in a black suit and white shirt. Having a fun, clever username adds some flair, like a purple checkered tie or pink nails with fancy designs on them. (Yes—those are my nails in the next picture. Like?)

Let's say you walked into a bookstore, and there was a book called *The Scientific Answers to Your Most Common Questions*. Would you buy it? Now, what if the title was instead *Why Do Men Have Nipples? Hundreds of Questions You'd Only Ask a Doctor After Your Third Martini*? Perhaps some of us, out of sheer embarrassment, would opt for the first choice, but I'm guessing that most of us would at least be intrigued by the scandalous title of the second choice . . . and then maybe go home and buy it online so no one can tell just how intrigued we are. (For the record, this is a real book. I own it. Don't judge.)

Now, back to usernames . . .

When dating online, one objective is to catch someone's attention quickly. There are so many options out there, so it's important to take every opportunity to differentiate yourself. As an exercise, think of two or three words that really define you—nouns, verbs, adjectives, anything. Then, try to string them together into a username. I'd much rather date a "Nats-FanFromAK" over a "283017390" any day. The first username has me curious. When did this person move from Alaska? And why would he then become a Nationals fan? (Don't get me wrong—I love my home team. I do wonder which team to root for, though, when the Nats play the Phillies, my former home team. At least I can get away with just wearing a red hat for both teams!) I've learned a lot about this "NatsFanFromAK" in a mere thirteen characters. If anything, your potential matches know that you put extra time and effort into the process to come up with something creative, even if it only took a minute. Let's also try to avoid anything negative, like "JustGotDumped" or "LonelyManHere."

Before you take the leap and post your username, though, make sure it doesn't have any undesired meanings that you didn't intend. For example, if you're from Virginia but cheer for New York football teams, you might want to stay away from something like "VAGiantsFan." Along those lines, if you're from Alabama, definitely avoid things like "AnALfan." Or how about "Buttongirl," who loves her collection of vintage buttons and brooches? It's probably best to leave anything that might be misconstrued as a body part out of your username. And lastly—the pièce de résistance—it might be a good idea to check your username in Urban Dictionary before you post it. There was a "tossed salad" incident on JDate that I don't want to happen to you.

Chapter 3

A BIG AND BOLD INTRO

Let's think about that same bookstore for a second. You remember, the one you walked into when buying *Why Do Men Have Nipples? Hundreds of Questions You'd Only Ask a Doctor After Your Third Martini*. After you read the title, you then read that first line on either the back of the book or the inside cover. What are you looking for? My guess is that you're looking for something to grab your attention, to suck you in. Would you rather buy a book with the line "This book is about a woman's adventure and coming of age" or one with the line "Read a rare tale about a woman's three-year trek through the Amazon to learn about love, hope, and passion" in it? I know which I'd buy, and I'd bet that you would, too.

On most of the dating sites, just a few words of your profile are initially shown. Someone needs to actively click on your profile to see the rest of it. For that reason, it's important to make the first sentence memorable in order to catch someone's attention and make him or her want to click in the first place.

Believe it or not, when perusing online dating profiles, people are often using the same criteria as those from that bookstore. I'm not saying that you have to include mystery, intrigue, and drama all within one sentence. In fact, drama is usually something people *do not* want to see in an online dating profile! What I am saying, though, is that you should consider the first line of your profile as a "hook." It should be something to draw people in. With so many people using online dating sites and so many profiles to weed through, it's best to take that one extra step to make sure you're catching someone's eye.

Below are some real examples from popular online dating sites of not so big and bold (a.k.a. boring) opening lines. And then I'll show a few examples that make the "big and bold" cut.

Yes, I am single. I am throwing it out there!

I sure hope you're single if you're on Match.com!

For the past few years, I've lived under the assumption that I'd meet someone in my normal circles of work, friends, and activities.

I'd say most people would have made that assumption. La dee da.

So . . . I have never done this online dating thing before, and I'm still on the fence about how I feel about it.

This one is not only boring, but it's also negative.

I work a lot, and I don't really have too many opportunities to meet new people.

On the surface, this line is not so bad since we all likely work too much these days, but by starting with this fact, it leads others to assume that the writer of this profile is a workaholic and has no time to date. Remember, people will infer things based on what you write, so make sure they infer correctly.

> So, I'm new to the city and thought that this might be a good way to meet people.

Again, while not horrible, this line doesn't really say much beyond the fact that she is new to the city.

> I enjoy life and like to have fun.

This is the worst! Raise your hand if you don't enjoy life and like to have fun. I better not see any hands raised!

Ready for the examples of some big and bold opening lines?

> Pick me, pick me! As a teacher, this phrase is all too familiar.

Not only does this line show that the online dater is a teacher, but it also shows that she has a sense of humor. Well done. She gets an A+.

> Being an engineer, the last time I wrote this profile, I approached it like a car engine . . . it functioned okay and got 32 miles per gallon, but it didn't attract women. (This was kind of a problem.)

He's able to make fun of himself. Many people see this as a very attractive quality in a partner since he doesn't take himself too seriously.

> I like extra salted buttered popcorn and malt balls at the movies.

She sounds like fun. Heck—I want to get to know her!

> I've lived in the US for over 30 years, but I still have my accent from where I grew up. Care to guess where?

This says so much—she's American but grew up abroad, so she's clearly fairly cultured. Plus, the question at the end adds a bit of intrigue, challenging the reader to guess where she's from. I'm thinking Australia.

> Most people say that they don't want drama in a relationship, right? But what if your partner is a theater teacher? I think I just found the loophole.

This is hysterical. Not only is it a commentary on dating, but it also shares what he does for a living and shows that he has a clever sense of humor.

> My mother used to say that I broke things just to see what would happen. She probably figured that out when, at five, I disassembled the chair she was sitting on and both she and the chair collapsed on top of me.

Can you guess that the profile writer became an engineer? She shows that her intellectual curiosity was present from the time she was little, and the profile goes on to show that she still maintains that curiosity today.

Even if two profiles were identical except for the first line, would you rather read one from the first grouping or one from the second? I would guess the latter. Don't let people pass you by simply because your first line bored them to sleep. Remember: When people go to the online dating bookstore, you want them to leave with your profile . . . or at least smile and send you an email to say hello.

Chapter 4

A POSITIVE ENDING

Have you ever read those profiles where the person sounds intelligent and generally interesting . . . until that fateful last line? I've seen them all:

Cowboys fans need not apply.

If you're looking for a fling, look the other way.

No drama, please!

If you're into country music, forget about it.

If you're a cat lover, move right along.

Don't write to me if you're not looking for a serious relationship.

Douchebags need not apply! (This was taken from someone's actual Match.com profile. I can't make this stuff up.)

In doing a quick search of Match.com for men ages 30 to 45 within 20 miles of my zip code, I found that 36 men used the expression "need not apply" somewhere in their profiles. And women, you may wonder? Over 100!

You might be thinking, "Is it really so bad to tell someone what I don't want?" Yes. Yes, it is. Let's take the cat statement above, for example. While I may not love cats, I'm definitely not into negativity, so I'll be turned off by a line eliminating a whole group of people for one seemingly silly trait. Instead, it's better to show people what you *do* want rather than what you don't. In this case, rather than calling your cat hatred to everyone's attention, just write about how you're looking for a dog lover because Fido is the main man in your life right now, and you'd like to change that. (For me, Scruffy is the little man of the house, and I wouldn't change that for a second.)

By including one of these lines about what you don't want in your profile, you come off as negative, or even bitter. "No drama, please" screams, "My last relationship was full of drama, and I am SO over that." "Douchebags need not apply" is not only a disgusting expression, but also says to someone, "This woman's been burned one too many times, and she is probably jaded about this whole dating thing."

Please take a moment to reread your profile, and if something comes off as negative, try to turn it into something positive. Let's take two examples:

Negative: Cowboys fans need not apply.

Positive: I love football, but you better be careful because I may have to tease you about your favorite team sometimes.

This line also serves as "email bait," enticing the reader to ask which team you like.

Negative: Don't write to me if you're not looking for a serious relationship.

Positive: I'm looking for someone who is ready for a meaningful (or committed) relationship.

That simple change makes a world of difference.

When people read about you, they are likely to remember the first thing (which we've already discussed) and the last thing you say, so make sure the end of your profile also comes across as confident, intelligent, and positive.

With that being said, it's still important that you list your deal-breakers. These are usually found in the "check-box questions," such as whether you're looking for a nonsmoker, someone of the same religion, etc.

An interesting situation happened to me last year that, at first glance, may not seem to relate to dating, but when you really think about it, it does.

Last summer, I went to adopt a dog. This was a big step for me since, as a young girl, I was bitten by my neighbor's dog and actually still have the scar to prove it. After months of petting dogs to get comfortable and reading *Dogs for Dummies* so I would have something of a clue after the pup joined the Ettin clan, I was ready to bite the bullet and adopt a puppy of my own. I searched the list on the dog rescue organization's website and fell in love with little Bashful's pictures. She was just so darn cute! I read her bio, and she seemed to have everything I was looking for—the right size, a good age, and that nice, brown, low-shedding fur that I like.

On that Sunday morning, I went to the adoption event, pages of notes in hand so I would know what to buy at the pet store once little Bashful was mine. (I'm an obsessive note-taker.) When I got there, she was just as cute as her photos . . . maybe even more so. And she was so sweet, walking right up to me and sitting in my lap. What more could I want?

So, I was told to go buy a collar while they got the paperwork ready. I opted to instead sit with Bashful for another few minutes before heading into the store, saying things like, "I'm going to be your puppy mommy." (I'm also a total sap.) As the forms were coming my way, and I was really starting to bond with my new friend, a supervisor came over to me and said (while Bashful was still in my lap, mind you), "We decided that we're not going to let you adopt this dog. She can only go to a home with other dogs. And by the way, she can't live in a big city, either." Had any of that been stated in her bio? No. Had they told me that before I started to get excited and bond with her? No. Would I have even looked twice at her had I known any of this was the case? Of course not. So I left, feeling sad that I was not getting the new best friend I wanted and deceived that something so important (a deal-breaker, if you will) had not been stated upfront.

As I walked away, I thought to myself that the situation

seemed oddly related to online dating. I'm sure we've all been in a situation where a profile says exactly what we want it to say. We meet our date and everything seems to be going fine until . . .

BAM! Your date tells you he doesn't want children.

BAM! She's really just separated and not divorced.

BAM! She has four kids, but she only listed one.

BAM! He said he's Jewish, but he's not practicing and doesn't care about his partner's religious affiliation. Yet, when I ordered a bacon-infused cocktail, it looked like he was going to have a heart attack.

In online dating, it's so important that your deal-breakers are out there front and center. If you don't want children, that's fine! Just make sure you check that box off in your profile. If you're extremely religious, that's fine, too! Don't underplay it simply to get more dates. The last thing you want is for someone to go out with you only to be disappointed because you didn't disclose something really important about yourself in your profile. So don't be bashful. Be true to yourself. You may go on fewer dates, but your dates will want you for who you really are rather than for the person who is trying to appeal to everyone simply by not sharing the truth.

This concept is important when searching for potential matches, too. As hard as it may be, try not to fall in love with someone's pictures and profile, which are just images and words on a page, before meeting in person. I kept that in mind as I continued to search for a pet. I wanted a dog who loved me for me—living in an apartment downtown, having no other pets (besides Sir Quackers, my childhood stuffed duck), and just wanting to shower him or her with love and affection. With that in mind, I rescued a different dog, Scruffy, from the same agency, and I could not be happier with him.

Q&A with Erika

Q: I realize a barrier to finding someone acceptable online is my age. Friends have encouraged me to lie about my age online because I look and behave much younger. Ridiculous! After writing to one guy, he responded, "I'm not looking for a 55-year-old divorced woman in Northern Virginia!" There is no way I would want to lie my way into a relationship with anyone. I realize that the same way I have an idea in my head as to what men of a certain age are all about, so do they about women. Therefore, if I am an active, vibrant, and youthful-looking woman of 55, I need to meet someone in person who won't judge me based upon my profile alone.
—Roseanne, 55, Fairfax, VA

A: I respect that you stood your ground with your friends regarding lying about your age. So many of my clients (most of them women) want to lie, and I always tell them that I don't condone it. Just as you said, it's never a good idea to start a relationship based on a lie. I agree 100% that the right man will love you for being you, no matter how old you are, and appreciate your 55 years of experience and wisdom!

Chapter 5

ASK QUESTIONS

Have you ever read those profiles that just seem to go on and on with no end in sight? It's like a long, self-indulgent soliloquy that you'd think was meant for performing a one-man show about someone's life rather than for trying to get a date.

Let's say you're at work and you're listening to a presentation on the merits of using LIFO (last-in, first-out) versus FIFO (first-in, first-out) accounting on last year's sales numbers. To me, this topic sounds fairly snooze-worthy (though I do remember those accounting terms from my first year in business school, so I guess I don't find it *that* boring). It would be nicer if the presenter engaged me somewhat more during the presentation. What if, for the accounting topic, rather than simply defining LIFO and FIFO (wake me up in an hour), the presenter started with the line, "Which carton of milk would you rather buy at the supermarket—the first one that was put on the shelf or the last?" That I might listen to! (Though, since supermarkets know this, they usually put the newer milk behind the older milk so that the older stuff sells first. If you can fit your arm into the back of that milk fridge at the store, which I'm generally too short to do, you might be rewarded with a few extra days of use . . . and your first ever milk-induced bruise.)

The same concept applies to online dating profiles. We'll talk about the length of a profile in the next chapter (it can, indeed, be too long), but for now, I'm going to suggest adding a question or two to your profile. This way, you're engaging the potential readers rather than boring them with your life story.

Again, it's best to assume, just like with the "interesting picture" we discussed earlier, that no one knows what to say to you in that first email simply because it's hard to figure out how to initiate communication. For that reason, you want to make it as easy as possible for people to write to you. Asking questions in your profile gives them a reason to write, even if that simply means answering your question. Even rhetorical questions work. Just as long as there's a well-placed question mark, you're good to go.

Let's look at some examples:

Just having finished my MBA, I'm making full use of my newfound free time. Want to join me?

This was actually from my very own online dating profile. It's a rhetorical question, but it lets prospective dates know that I'm truly looking for someone to join me on my adventure.

When I'm not pounding the pavement on a training run, you can find me trying a new restaurant in the city. Any good recommendations?

This question could lead to so many wonderful responses. In fact, a client of mine who used a similar line received so many recommendations (and dates, of course) that she didn't know what to do with all of them. Good problems, my friends, good problems.

> I think brunch is one of the best inventions ever made. Don't you agree?

Sticking with the food theme, while seemingly rhetorical, this question could actually elicit some pretty funny responses, such as, "I actually think brunch is kind of odd. Maybe I just don't like the thought of having a burger and an omelet on the same side of the menu!" or "I completely agree. My favorite day of the week is Sunday since it's perfectly acceptable to sit at brunch for three hours over both a coffee and a mimosa. Do you have a favorite place in town?"

> My boss once called me groovy and green, so I guess I'll go with that. I like to hike and practice yoga, I enjoy the Environmental Film Fest, and I'm giving the whole vegetarian thing a try. Now that I think about it, I guess he wasn't too far off, was he?

This is a perfect example of engaging the reader to actually think about what she's said. Nice work. And she does sound pretty "groovy and green" to me.

Remember the point of the online dating profile—to catch someone's attention and ultimately meet in person. What better way is there to do that than to ask a question? (See what I did there?)

Chapter 6

CHECK THE LENGTH

Most of us remember the story of *Goldilocks and the Three Bears*, where the porridge, chairs, and beds weren't quite what anyone was looking for . . . until they were "just right." Is it possible for an online dating profile to have a "just right" length as well? You bet.

What is too short for a profile, and what is too long? As a general rule of thumb, just a few sentences would make for a profile that is too short, but anything over about three medium-length paragraphs is too long. With a too-short profile, people may assume that you're not invested in the process because you didn't put the necessary time into filling out your profile. And with a too-long profile, people will simply see the excessive length, think, "I don't have time to read this," and click on someone else's more succinct profile instead. No need to tell your life story. Save it for the date. And even then, use some discretion!

Let's look at a few examples taken from actual online dating sites:

TOO SHORT (28-YEAR-OLD MALE)

> I'm looking for someone who makes me laugh at myself
> and at the world. I am spontaneous and am up for anything,
> dancing the night away or just hanging out and spending
> time together. Simple things make me happy.

At least this person was honest about simple things making him happy . . . including his profile! What did we learn about this person? Nothing. It's too short and doesn't give us any insight into who this person really is.

TOO LONG (57-YEAR-OLD MALE)

Note: I cleaned this one up a bit for obvious grammatical errors, though there are still some style choices I would not make. Namely, I love the Oxford comma. Apparently he's on the fence about it, considering his inconsistency. Feel no obligation to read it in its entirety. In fact, I would highly recommend against it.

> They say if you look and look, you won't find her. But,
> since I am at a point where I can actually say that I'm
> ready for that special person to be in my life, I just can't
> resist the temptation. So, is she ready to meet that
> great guy, who's caring, attentive and loving? A genuine
> sweetie who loves his family, friends and life. More about
> me? Well, I stay active and take good care of myself,
> physically, mentally and spiritually. For fun? I'm a native
> [of the area] trying to finally take advantage of what

this great city has to offer. So, I enjoy trying out different restaurants, concerts and picnics, walks through the zoo and the museums. I also enjoy biking down the trails, hiking, taking in a show, going to sporting events (season ticket holder here). Being somewhat civic minded, I volunteer when I can, working with needy people or with kids. Even if it's something as simple as cooking or handing out food at a shelter for a few hours, it's a great feeling for me. I am quite multifaceted in my interests, as you can see. Just as comfy sipping a glass of fine red wine at a nice restaurant as I am sipping a bottle of fine cold beer at a sports bar. I also like the quiet evenings at home. Just staying in and cooking dinner (and yes, I can cook!), watching a movie and cuddling. As for romance, well, I love it. I'm very affectionate when I am with someone who's special to me. A real sucker for romance. How many guys will actually admit that? Love hand holding, long hugs, playing with hair and snuggling. I believe that affection is one of the best ways to express yourself—to tell someone you think that she's special. And, I can say it using words too. I always remember the special days— holidays, birthdays, anniversaries, and milestones. So, is there someone out there looking for a great guy, who's looking for a sweetheart he can treat like gold? I'm very interested in meeting someone who would like to enjoy some fun times and romance with me. Yes, I am hopeful that it will ultimately lead to something deeper, but going on some fun dates would be a good place to start. Want to be my playmate/partner/best bud and take part in some awesome activities? Like fun dinners out (and in), sharing nice wine, going to movies, museums and more. Plus, I'm also interested in going to the theater or sporting events. It really would be great to enjoy these fun times with someone. Preferably someone who's kind hearted, open-minded, genuine and down to earth. The nice/kind to a fault type of people appeal to me. Honesty, trustworthiness, open communication and playfulness are necessities. And, I have a lot of respect for ladies who are witty and intelligent. If you're opinionated and unafraid to speak your mind, that's just fine. I can certainly deal with that. I'll probably find it refreshing. Please, no game players, liars or inconsiderate people. I want to be around someone who enjoys the sophisticated fun once in a while and the low key, laid back moments as well. She'll be accepting and appreciative of the person I am. I'm looking for someone who enjoys receiving attention from a very romantic, affectionate guy. Hand holding, hugs, snuggling. And, she occasionally has to let me spoil her and shower endless attention and affection on her—by letting me brush her hair, polish her toenails, give her massages or just cuddle with her for hours. She'll enjoy getting silly and playful with me from time to time. More than anything, she will be my best friend and listen to me when I need to vent, not fault me too harshly for my shortcomings, will offer advice and solutions to dealing with the day to day battles of life in general. Does team sound so unromantic? Not to me. That's what I'm looking for. A teammate, a partner, best friend in the world. Please, be OK with taking things a little slow—at first.

Wow. Honestly, this guy could have won the Nobel Prize and cured the world of famine, but no one would know because people won't read it. It's just too long. After returning from a long day of work, it's a daunting task to read a profile like this, so most people simply won't. Don't give your potential dates the opportunity to pass you by simply because their attention span runs shorter than your profile. Also, a long profile seems fairly self-indulgent, as if you find yourself to be so important that you *must* share every little detail with the world. Don't get me wrong—I also like myself—but it's not necessary to list every accomplishment, trait, and hobby in the profile. Leave something to talk about on the date.

JUST RIGHT

Example 1 (52-year-old female):

I like my chocolate dark, my puppy white and fluffy, and my family nearby. Being the mother to a sports-playing son (we have a lot of shoes in the house) and a college-bound daughter certainly keeps me on my toes, but I'm looking forward to taking a step back and earning some well-deserved "me" time. When I do get to carve that time out, I love anything outdoors, including hiking, biking, going to the beach, and just enjoying nature. Once you've lived in Hawaii and Vancouver, you're a bit spoiled by having natural beauty right at your doorstep. Music is another passion of mine, and while I like the symphony and the opera (and have taught my kids early to appreciate it), I also like a little bit of country. I promise not all country songs are about keying your boyfriend's car and pickup trucks . . . just the good ones.

I'm looking for someone open-minded (especially about my having a family), fun-loving, and intelligent. For me, nothing is more attractive than intelligence . . . and a nice smile doesn't hurt, either. Ideally, we'll each have a passion for something, no matter what it is, and will be thrilled to let each other in on the secret of what makes us each who we are. Ready to start our adventure?

Example 2 (34-year-old male):
When I was five, I was always a fan of that Snickers commercial where you'd see a man reach into a bag of peanuts, grab a handful, close his fist, and re-open his hand to magically show a large-size Snickers bar. Thinking that this was reality (seems plausible, right?), I tried the same on my end but was disappointed to find that no such Snickers bar appeared. Some may call this naïve . . . I like to call it positive thinking.

That same positive thinking has carried over to the rest of my life in slightly more mature ways: I left a job in finance to potentially make a difference in the world by studying public health, I'm a die-hard Cal football fan even when they're not doing so great, and as much as I love my life in sunny LA, having gone to grad school on the East Coast has made me so much more well-rounded as a person.

The consultant in me decided that bulleting a few other things would be the easiest:

- I make a mean pesto/potato-crusted salmon, and if you put me in front of a grill, I'm a happy guy.
- I may or may not have read all of the Harry Potter books . . . and liked them.
- While I might take a minute to warm up to new people, once I get to know you, everything's on the table.
- I lived in Omaha once for 15 months. Definitely an interesting experience.
- I could eat sushi for breakfast, lunch, and dinner if that was deemed socially acceptable.

Example 3 (39-year-old female):

I'm the kind of woman who will adapt to whatever situation I'm put in, who will remember your parents' birthdays, who will buy snowshoes for Snowmageddon (oh wait—I did that), and who is really sweet and warm but can also be a tough cookie if she wants to be.

You can often find me doing something outdoors—hiking with my dog Rex, traveling the US, camping, or kayaking (I own one . . . still working on getting the helmet and oar). I like to think I'm a rugged adventurer! But I'm also a covert geek who likes to watch The History Channel and read books about psychology so I can understand different types of people better. Everything in moderation, right?

Are you the type of guy who lives by his word? Do you like to work out, but have a nice balance between working out and living? And more importantly, are you open to trying new and fun things together? If so, we might just be a great match. And while I consider myself to be pretty independent, having a door opened for me still makes me smile.

I wrote these last three profiles for my clients, and they all had much success with them, especially the last woman, who met someone online using this profile and dated him for over two years. Notice that all of these profiles engage the reader, ask questions, and hold our attention from the beginning to the end by being the right length. These profiles are not too short since we were able to learn a lot about each person, but they are also not too long and won't intimidate someone with excessive length.

Chapter 7

PROVIDE DETAILS
AND SPECIFICS

So this weekend, he made sure to tell me that I was the only person he was seeing, that I am the only person he wants to see in the future and smacked a huge kiss on me. The past several days have been extremely emotionally intimate and exciting. After dinner, he pulled out my computer and his and said, "Let's do this! Let's have our cancellation ceremony tonight!" So . . . we hit the button together. Long story short, things are going well and the future is looking bright. Thank you again for all the support—I am not done sharing.

—Katie, 36, Charlotte, NC

Let's say we're in a room full of 100 people at a networking event or a happy hour. Before knowing a thing about anyone else, we are all basically the same—just people in a room together. Now, what if we try to segment the 100 people into categories? For example, we might ask whether anyone in the room likes to cook. Let's say that 25 people raise their hands to indicate that they enjoy cooking. Now these 25 people are different from the other 75, who would rather jump into a pool of crocodiles than try to decipher a recipe in *Joy of Cooking*. Those 25 people, though, are now all the same in that they like to cook. So let's delve a bit further by asking around to see what specific dishes these people like to cook:

Erika: "I love making my grandma's kugel recipe with apricots and raisins."

As an aside, kugel is a Jewish noodle pudding, and the recipe I still use to this day was passed down to me from my Grandma Henny, my dad's mom. Sadly, Grandma passed away several years ago after a long and hard battle with Alzheimer's disease. After she stopped cooking, I took on the role of being the family kugel chef for holidays and gatherings. Every time Grandma Henny ate my kugel, she would say, "Erika, this kugel is delicious! Where did you get the recipe?" And I, of course, responded, "Grandma, it's yours!" While Alzheimer's is a terrible thing to watch progress in someone you love, I always have to smile when I think of Grandma and her kugel.

Joyce: "I make my stuffed cabbage every year around Thanksgiving since it's my daughters' favorite dish."

Lisa: "I make an excellent eggplant dish, especially when I use my pepper-infused olive oil."

Marty: "All I know how to make is a tuna melt. But it's a good tuna melt, if I do say so myself!"

Elyse: "I'm no gourmet chef or anything, but I do love making homemade pizza."

The five of us have now differentiated ourselves, first from the larger group because we each like to cook, and now from the 25-person subset because we have shared specifically what we enjoy cooking. Would you rather go on a date with someone who says he likes to cook or someone who says he makes the best apple pie on this side of the Mississippi? Unless you hate apple pie (who hates apple pie!?), then I'd venture to say the latter.

In your online dating profile, it's very important to differentiate yourself to the point where people can see you for you and not assume you're just like everyone else. Let's look at these two profile excerpts:

I love to laugh and have fun. My family and friends are so important to me, and I always try to be there for them when I can. I love to cook, run, and play with my dog.

♥ ♥ ♥

When I'm not chasing my dog all the way to the dog park every morning (trust me—he's fast!), I love hosting family and friends for dinner. It gives me great pride to make my late grandma's kugel recipe for every holiday. The best advice she ever gave to me was to use a whole stick of butter every time. Maybe it's a good thing I get my exercise by running every morning . . . even if I can never catch Scruffy!

The first profile doesn't tell us much. It lists a few hobbies, but on the whole, it's pretty nondescript. The second profile, however, really gives us a sense of who this person is—someone silly and family oriented who loves to cook and who has an abnormally fast dog. That's someone people likely want to meet.

So look around the room, and if you think you might be writing the same profile as the person next to you, especially if that person is a stranger, then it's time to get more specific. There's an art to setting yourself apart online, and now you're well equipped with some ideas for how to do it.

In addition to setting yourself apart by digging into the details, there's one more thing I'd like to call to your attention: **The Curse of the Empty Adjective**.

- I'm smart, funny, and attractive.
- I'm humble, successful, and kind.
- I'm romantic, thoughtful, and trustworthy.
- I'm sexy, passionate, and fearless.
- I'm compassionate, honest, and friendly.

How many times have we seen lines like these in online dating profiles? If I had a nickel for every time I saw what I call an "empty adjective," I'd be a very rich woman. What is an empty adjective? It's a word that you use to describe yourself that can't be proven until someone gets to know you. For example, I might say that I'm funny, but how would you know if that's the truth? Maybe I'm funny to some people (the ones who love puns and wordplay) but not to others. Or maybe my definition of being honest is telling someone she has a wad of spinach stuck in her teeth, but your definition is giving back the extra penny the cashier accidentally gave to you at Whole Foods last week. A long time ago, I dated someone for six months who said in his online dating profile, "I'm really romantic." Was he? Not in the least. The curse of the empty adjective strikes again.

This is where the concept of "show, don't tell" really comes into play. For example, rather than saying that you're funny, say something that you actually find funny instead. That way, you're not only getting your point across, but you're differentiating yourself from everyone else who also simply states, "I'm funny," or worse, "My friends tell me I'm funny." The latter is just a way to say the same thing while attempting to be humble. Sadly, it doesn't work.

Let's think of a story for some of the adjectives just mentioned:

Friendly: I tend to walk into a room and immediately ask people's names—the cashier at The Container Store, the security guard at my building, the parking attendant at school, the lady who slices the bread at the supermarket. I may not remember them all, but I always ask.

Fearless: Despite my fear of flying, I knew I had to go to India as my culminating trip for business school. I may or may not have hyperventilated a bit. And then I realized, "I can do this!" Since then, I've been to 12 countries in the last four years.

Trustworthy: It wasn't until many years after college that I realized everyone on my dorm floor had put me down as their emergency contact. They must have really trusted me . . . or knew I'd have nothing else going on!

Funny: I'm a dog lover, especially when it comes to my wise old dachshund. Unfortunately, he doesn't enjoy dining out quite as much as I do (he likes the leftovers, though), he can't read the subtitles of the documentaries I watch, he can't help me with that pesky last letter of the crossword puzzle, and when it comes to dancing, well, he has two left feet . . . literally.

Words like attractive, sexy, young-looking, and fit don't need to be stated at all because someone can decide that for himself or herself simply by looking at the photos you post.

These empty adjectives will get glossed over and end up having the opposite effect of what you want—they'll become meaningless. Remember: Be sure to set yourself apart and not get caught in the . . . *dun dun dun* . . . curse of the empty adjective.

Chapter 8

ANSWER THE EXTRA QUESTIONS

Almost every online dating site has some additional questions to answer to bolster the "About Me" section. On Match.com, for example, these include "Favorite Hot Spots," "Favorite Things," "For Fun," and "Last Read." The purpose of these extra sections is to allow users to provide a bit more detail to the reader. For example, I might respond, "Hummus and pita chips, my dog Scruffy, the color pink, my tap shoes, a microphone and a stage, my job helping people with online dating, tomato bisque, and muffins" to the question asking what my favorite things are. (They are all true, by the way.) I have just provided someone with so much "email bait" that it should be a piece of cake (double chocolate, please) to find something to say in that first email.

Other sites, such as OkCupid, ask a lot of additional questions, more than just the four I mentioned above. There is no need to answer all of them (remember to check the length), but do make sure you respond to the ones where you feel you can write creative, unique answers. I rarely have clients answer the "Typical Friday Night" question because

90 percent of the time, the answer is, "Relaxing after a long work week," which really doesn't tell us much, if anything, about the person who wrote the profile.

Section 3

BE YOURSELF . . .
EVERYONE ELSE IS TAKEN

In this section, you'll learn:

- How to make yourself stand out from the crowd
- Why it's okay to turn some people off in your profile
- Which kinds of profiles get the most positive attention
- Why you should stop hiding your quirks and start reveling in them

Chapter 9

TURN SOME PEOPLE OFF

Thanks again for the great profile! Friends have said that you did an amazing job of capturing my personality! Plus, even though it's only been up for a few days, the positive response has been dramatic!

—Megan, 28, Victoria, British Columbia

Hopefully the advice in this book will make things a bit easier, but even if you're a professional writer, when it comes to putting pen to paper about yourself (or fingers to keyboard, as the case may be), that's where things get a bit trickier.

Many people immediately think to themselves, "I should write exactly what I think people want to hear. I want lots of people to be interested in me, after all!" I beg to differ. While of course it's nice to be liked, you don't want to lose yourself in the process of trying to fit into some arbitrary mold that you think others want to see. For example, take the lines, "I'm just as comfortable in a little black dress and heels as I am in jeans and flip-flops," and "I'm just as happy out on the town as I am at home with a movie and a glass of wine on the couch." Do these lines actually tell us anything? No. They simply cover all the bases. To me, they read, "I am trying to show you that I'm versatile so that I don't turn anyone off or exclude anyone."

While it may seem counterintuitive, I'll come right out and say it: It's okay to turn people off in your profile! It's more important to be the real you, not the version of yourself you think people want to see, and not the version of yourself who attempts to appeal to every single person on the site. Just be yourself. That way, you know when someone shows interest, it's because he or she likes the actual things you said, not just the fact that you were being inclusive.

It's okay if you don't run marathons, ski, travel to Antarctica, skydive, or camp. I don't, either. I personally would choose playing trivia, riding the stationary bike at the gym, shopping online for shoes, or even doing a crossword puzzle over camping any day of the week. A bit nerdy? Perhaps. The real me? Absolutely. So if someone out there is a hard-core camper and wants to sleep in a tent every weekend, then we wouldn't be a good fit, and I'd rather we know that from the get-go. In my old online dating profile, the first line was, "I think puns are a sign of intelligence . . . or maybe that's just me rationalizing how often I make them." If someone cringes at the thought of *fowl* play on Thanksgiving or doesn't care that carrying a lot of pennies just makes *cents*, that's okay. He just wouldn't be the right person for me.

I have a challenge for you: After you've followed all of

the advice here and written your online dating profile, give it an additional read-through and see if it contains one of the "all-inclusive" lines. If it does, change it into something that better represents who you really are. Remember that it's okay to share your interests in bird-watching, chess-playing, beer-making, and whatever else you do for fun. Yes, you may (and likely will) turn someone off. But you may just turn exactly the right person on.

Chapter 10

DON'T JUDGE YOURSELF

I'm a lawyer. It's true. But I promise I'm not a typical one!

I guess you've noticed that I'm a vegetarian, but don't worry—I won't get upset if you order a big, juicy steak in front of me.

Even though I have to get up early for work (at 5:15 a.m.), I swear that doesn't mean I can't stay up past 10:00 p.m.

How many times have you seen lines like this in someone's profile? Perhaps you even have one like this in yours. The common theme here is that the author is compensating for (and judging) something in his or her own life that is *assumed* to be a turn-off. Seemingly innocuous lines like these can actually be very off-putting for someone reading your profile, because hiding underneath the "but," "don't worry," and "I swear" is a thinly veiled sense of insecurity.

Let's take the first line, for example, about the woman who is a lawyer. (As a side note, this is no commentary on how I feel about lawyers. In fact, my dad is a lawyer, and he's the best dad around.) In this example, the person writing this profile—let's call her Shelby—assumes that her occupation could be a deal-breaker for her online dating soul mate and immediately tries to compensate for that fact. But what she's actually doing is buying into the (mostly untrue) stereotype that people dislike lawyers. Shelby thinks that the second someone reads her profile, he will dismiss her because of this one attribute. But rather than being turned off by the fact that she's a lawyer (and an impressive one at that), many people will instead be turned off by the fact that she presumes to already know how they feel about it.

In addition, Shelby is calling more attention to something that may not play a large role, or any role, in someone's decision-making process. By saying, "I'm not a typical one," she has not only called attention to her job, but she has also made it the focus of her profile. Is that her sole defining factor? She's essentially saying, "My job defines me, but please don't hold this against me."

As most of us know, online dating can be pretty daunting, and writing the profile is perhaps the scariest part. There's so much uncertainty, and people are often very uncomfortable with uncertainty.

What if people assume I have no life outside of work?

What if they think I will always argue until they agree with me?

What if they decide I'm a total nerd because I go to a weekly law discussion group called the "Legal Eagles," and we all wear shirts with the scales of justice on them? (Okay, maybe that one is warranted.)

Instead of dealing with this uncertainty, Shelby would prefer to assume that we already have these preconceived notions about lawyers rather than leave it up to chance that someone may not care, or perhaps more likely, absolutely love the fact that she's a successful lawyer. What they won't love is that she's downplaying it. So don't judge yourself. Own it, be confident, and then move on.

I'm a lawyer.

I'm a vegetarian.

I wake up at an ungodly hour every morning.

How did your potential future dates react? Who cares? Don't assume they feel a certain way. All you did was state the truth. Leave the rest up to the powers that be.

Chapter 11

BE YOURSELF (IN CASE YOU FORGOT ALREADY)

Wow, what an excellent profile. Very well-written, but also very approachable. Brava! One thing I find particularly impressive is that it really sounds like me. The self-deprecating line you added about my hair is the kind of thing I often say at the store. When I buy a bunch of heavy stuff, they will say, "Do you need help with that?" I will often reply, "No, thank you. I'm stronger than I look" and then pause and add with a smile "but not *that* much stronger." I am glad you also captured my general geekiness—hopefully easier to see in my emails than in person, but they are both part of "the magic that is me," as Frasier Crane would say.

—Tony, 45, Alexandria, VA

Let's start with a blank canvas. First, we'll draw me at a trivia night or a Scotch tasting. Then, we'll add a heart to the picture since I'm a dating coach. And finally, let's paint on a big smile since it's a permanent fixture on my face.

Now, let's paint my friend Cassie. She has an oven mitt on since she's an excellent baker. And then we'll add a sheepish grin because she has a playful and sometimes clumsy side. Lastly, we can't forget her alarm clock because she gets up at 5:00 a.m. for work every day. (Maybe she'd get along well with that other early bird we just mentioned!)

These two pictures look pretty different, right?

Now, I'd like to describe myself:

> I'm a fit, intelligent, and attractive person who likes to have fun. My family and friends are the most important people in my life, and I'm lucky to be surrounded by great people. I would love the opportunity to travel more and find the time to see the world. I like to get out and have a good time but also enjoy a night in with dinner and a movie. I would love to meet someone who makes me laugh, knows how to treat people right, and doesn't take himself too seriously.

Okay, Cassie—your turn:

> I'm a fit, intelligent, and attractive person who likes to have fun. My family and friends are the most important people in my life, and I'm lucky to be surrounded by great people. I would love the opportunity to travel more and find the time to see the world. I like to get out and have a good time but also enjoy a night in with dinner and a movie. I would love to meet someone who makes me laugh, knows how to treat people right, and doesn't take himself too seriously.

Wow! We are so different, yet we sound exactly the same. It's amazing . . . or is it? When you peruse the online dating sites, many of the profiles say some variation of the exact same thing. (I actually took this profile directly from Match.com as I was searching for a client recently.) What did I learn about this person? Nothing. It's actually pretty remarkable—this could be me, and this could be Cassie. Could it be you, too?

In online dating, differentiating yourself is the key. You want someone to be able to paint a picture of *you* in his or her mind rather than painting a generic person who could be just about anyone.

Some common phrases to avoid are:

I am funny. The same goes for smart, loyal, fun, etc.

As we discussed before, actually say something funny or smart, and give an anecdote as to how you're loyal or fun.

I like to work hard, and I like to play hard.

What does this really mean? I hope you work hard at work, and I also hope you enjoy your free time.

I can't believe I'm doing this.

We're all in the same boat. It's no secret. And you've just made the reader feel like he or she should be ashamed of doing online dating.

It's hard to write about yourself.

There's absolutely no need to point out the obvious. That line is just wasting precious space in your profile.

I'm really spontaneous and open-minded.

When we describe our friends, do we really say, "Wow—she is so . . . spontaneous, isn't she?" Also, these adjectives can mean different things to different people.

I'm just as comfortable in a dress (or tux) as I am in jeans and flip-flops.

We already discussed this one and its artificial inclusiveness. It's better to share what you like to do and where you like to go versus trying to appeal to the masses.

Let's try this again. Cassie, please describe yourself:

My 10th-grade cooking teacher told me I was unique— maybe she was right! When I'm not at work, you can often find me baking (I guess she did influence me a little), waking up with the sun, or riding the bike at the gym while reading *The Wall Street Journal*. I've been lucky enough to visit five countries in the last two years, and next on the list is Argentina. Interested in learning the tango? I also love trying new restaurants, especially if Pad Thai is involved.

I'd like to find someone who takes his work seriously and has goals in life but knows how to loosen his tie at the end of the day with a Guinness in hand and some football on in the background. Go Terps!

This person is unique. This person is quirky. This person has idiosyncrasies. Now we have a beautiful, one-of-a-kind picture on our canvas. I'll take it!

Section 4

WHAT NOT TO DO

In this section, you'll learn:

- What to avoid in your online dating profile
- Which phrases turn people off
- What minor things you can do to attract
  more people

Just as important as learning what to write in your online dating profile is learning what not to write. Many people actually have a lot of great material, yet they insert something that turns people off. This can negate a lot of the redeeming qualities about the profile.

Chapter 12

GRAMMAR MATTERS

If you know me (everyone reading this book is now in this category—congratulations!), then you know that I have major grammar pet peeves. Don't even get me started on the Oxford comma, which you already know I'm a huge fan of, or the correct use of past participles. I definitely fear that text messaging is taking over the world in a grammatically negative way, and if one more person skips the apostrophe in "let's," I may just scream.

Okay, back to business. When you're putting yourself out there in the vast online dating pool, it's important to take the time to read and reread your profile to make sure that "your" not messing up easy words and hurting your chance to find the perfect match. Robert H. Thaler and Cass R. Sunstein, the authors of the book *Nudge* (which has nothing to do with my business, as it happens, but is an excellent book), point out that it's often the important decisions—the 401(k) and the health care plan—that get overlooked, while we spend more time and energy doing the much smaller tasks. As they observe, " . . . 58 percent [of those in their survey] spent less than one hour determining both their contribution rate and investment decisions [for their 401(k)]. Most people spend more time than that picking a new tennis racket or television set."[2] Thaler and Sunstein also note that once the investment decision is made, the choices are rarely, if ever, looked at again. I don't know about you, but I definitely spend more time making vacation plans (remember that cruise?) than I do looking over my IRA statement every month. Guilty as charged.

The same sad fact is true for online dating. Many people think that writing an online dating profile is something to quickly rush through in order to post it immediately, and they rarely change it during their tenure on an online dating site. As we've talked about before, this is one thing that you really should spend your time on. You're putting yourself out there for the world to see, so you might as well put your best foot forward. When was the last time you even read what you wrote in your profile that fateful day when you signed up for an online dating site? If you can't remember, or if you have to look back at your profile when someone sends an email referencing something in it, then it's been too long.

When you're finally done writing your profile—having spent the appropriate amount of time on it, of course—I can't stress enough the importance of getting yourself an "unpaid intern" (a friend, sibling, parent, etc.) to read through it just in case you missed anything.

Oftentimes, just as with texting, the language of online dating gets mangled. It's like we have a new vocabulary, one that wouldn't make our high school English teachers proud. I don't know about you, but I probably wouldn't go out with a reformed "cereal dater" (I prefer oatmeal), someone who rides the "stationery" bike (to write thank you notes?), or someone who wants an "intellagent" partner (hmm).

As a final word, do remember that no one is perfect. Maybe your new beau or babe will be a terrible speller but will be great at storytelling, identifying different kinds of butterflies based on their wingspan, or calculating mathematical integrals. Everyone is smart in a different way, so it's important to decide if some initial "flaw" is really a deal-breaker for you. Either way, give your profile the final once-over just in case, because no one wants to go out with someone who is "humerus"—arms just aren't that funny.

Chapter 13

LET'S TALK ABOUT SEX

In this day and age, sex runs rampant throughout TV, movies, and generally every aspect of pop culture. Some TV shows (*Sex and the City* was a personal favorite), songs, and plenty of movies go into far more detail than I care to. (Remember the good ol' days when the men and women slept in separate twin beds in the same room? That still makes me chuckle.)

When it comes to looking for a serious, committed relationship online, however, sex and your online dating profile should not mix. Consider the two like oil and water, pickles and ice cream, toothpaste and orange juice . . . you get the idea. In its most innocuous form, people imply sex in countless profiles that mention touching each other and cuddling by the fire. While cuddling by the fire may sound lovely indeed, your profile is meant for you to talk about your hobbies and personality and what you're looking for in a partner. Who doesn't like a romantic cuddle session? All that line serves to do is take up extra space on the page when you could be using that prime real estate to win someone over with your wit and charm. I don't know about you, but I personally wouldn't want someone I don't know creating a visual image of me cuddling on the couch in my cozy polka-dotted pajamas and comfy slippers. Creepy!

Then there is the other extreme: explicitly mentioning sex in your profile. Unless you're looking for a predominantly physical relationship (which, of course, some people are), mentioning sex is an easy way to turn someone off who might have otherwise been interested in you.

Below are some **real, unedited examples,** taken from multiple online dating sites, of profiles where the "sex talk" is simply self-defeating:

I like fishing and travel and sex.

This was the first line of a man's profile!

I recently ended a faithful, 12-year marriage because I was unhappy with the intimacy and sex.

This is certainly none of our business. It also makes the reader question whether she would live up to his seemingly high standards in the intimacy and sex department.

To be clear, uninhibited intimacy means I want a woman who enjoys cuddling up, flirting, talking dirty, and giggling in the arms of a man. I want a woman who simply loves having sex with a man. I want a woman who enjoys receiving oral sex . . .

It went downhill from here. I spared your eyes—trust me.

I think it is important for the sake of compatibility, so I am leading with this: as it turns out, I prefer to be somewhat dominant in the bedroom. So yeah. There it is. I just wrote that, just put it right out there lol. :)

Is his name Christian Grey? If not, then this line is completely inappropriate.

> I am looking for someone who is as ambitious as I am and has strong morals and family values. Someone who shares the same goals in life as I do. Oh yeah, and the sex has to be great too!

This one starts out with such promise. Too bad it doesn't end that way. (This one was written by a woman, by the way.)

> Simple down to earth, compassionate, confident, romantic and loves to see ladies in nicely fitted tight/painted on jeans look.

This is a more subtle, yet still pretty graphic, way of implying something sexual.

> When dating, I like to spend Sundays in bed making love. I tend to think I am okay at it. I am also generously endowed, it's not just short, African American guys that have it going on down there. This white guy can hang.

I couldn't make this stuff up if I tried. These lines are so wrong on so many levels. And if you're going to be that disgusting and politically incorrect, at least write in proper sentences!

Sex is an intimate thing to be shared between two consenting adults, not an entire online dating community. So try to leave the "sex talk" in your mind and off your profile. It's not until you know someone well enough that you should invite him or her to hear your thoughts and eventually participate in them.

Chapter 14

SUMMARY OF WHAT NOT TO DO

Throughout this book, I have doled out advice and tips for successful profile-writing, so when a rare gem comes across that's so good—and by good, I actually mean horribly, pathetically bad—and goes against every piece of advice I could ever give, I feel that it's my duty to share it with my readers. Remember, this is an example of **what not to do**. Without losing its integrity, I've even taken out a whole paragraph from this profile. The rest is copied verbatim.

I'm more of a "journey" than a "destination" sort of guy so let me kick this off with a little narrative snapshot of what went down during the past couple of months in my world so you can get a sense of what made me the man I am today. In October, I moved [here] to start my first real job ever: baby corporate lawyer at a giant, multi-national law firm. The expectation was that I'd order dinner into the office and take dial cars home with alarming frequency because I'd be working so hard. I wasn't exactly happy about this, but I was also excited to take on the challenge of actual responsibility after so many years studying things that were supposed to prepare me for it. I saw no reason to give up on finding some sort of work/life balance before I'd even tried. After all, lots of lawyers (not to mention other professionals) have worked that hard before and continue to do so routinely. Total immersion in whatever it is you happen to be doing teaches you things about the structure and implications of that which would never register during a mere dalliance. I was genuinely looking forward to learning all these secrets about how the world works and contributing to something larger than myself, and maybe figuring what I might like to do with the rest of my life (or just the next couple of years) in the process. I always try to accentuate the positive.

Anyway, it really didn't work out. Because of forces beyond my control or comprehension, I spent most of those first few months sitting on my ass and reading on the internet about the outside world where people actually did things for a living. I also played a lot of Facebook Scrabble . . . Things are starting to pick up a little now, but it also turns out that corporate law is nowhere near as cool as I hoped it might be and it doesn't look like there's much I can do about it if I work harder. Oh well. Sometimes things don't go as planned, but that's part of the fun!

I also had a girlfriend for most of the period described above and my relationship with her was much more important than any frustrations I felt about the futility of my job. We have since parted ways amicably. Hence, online dating.

It just took me, like, 1000 characters to draw the

profound confusion [sic] that I joined an online dating site to try and meet girls. Amazing. In my defense, I studied literature in college and wanted to be a writer when I was younger (who can remember?) so I sometimes make things a little more complicated and overwrought than they need to be. I'm no drama king, though. It's only for the aesthetics . . . did I make you smile?

The main problems:

- Too long: As we discussed earlier, a few sentences will not be enough to show who you are, but anything over about three paragraphs is much too long. People will simply see the length and think, "I don't have time to read this after a long day of work," and click on someone else's profile. Remember, there is simply no need to tell your life story. Save it for the date . . . and even then, leave something to the imagination!

- Too negative: No one wants to date a Negative Nellie, so stay away from talking about bad times in your life and ex-girlfriends or ex-boyfriends (or ex-spouses). People will think, "You hate your job and you just broke up with your girlfriend. What's next for this guy?"

- Too busy: We all have busy jobs, but leading with that unfortunate circumstance is not the way to go because it only leads to one question: Does he even have time to date?

Profiles are not supposed to be a stream of consciousness narrative about your life story. He would even have been better off using the worst line out there—I love to laugh and have fun—and nothing else.

GATHER AROUND . . . IT'S STORY TIME!

Note to Selfie

Sometime last year, I was working from home, and Scruffy looked at me and started to bark. I've learned my lesson that if Scruffy barks, I should take him out. Sometimes it means he wants to play, and sometimes it means he lost his green ball under the couch, but after he had an accident once after he barked at me, I don't risk it anymore.

So, I took him out, and while I was outside, I came across this extremely good-looking guy I had never seen before walking a dog. I decided to start chatting with this guy. We made some small talk, and I asked him if he lived in my building. He said that he didn't and that he was temporarily doing some dog-walking between jobs before he was to leave for a year on a detail for the government . . . or something like that. We exchanged first names, and then he went inside to drop the dog off. (I also happened to look really cute that day, in a short black skirt, boots, and tights. He liked what he saw, I found out.)

Like I said, he was really quite attractive, and I figured that since he didn't live in my building, he had to come back out at some point after dropping the dog off, right? So, I decided to basically pace with Scruffy outside my apartment building until he came out. I even told a neighbor what I was doing since I looked ridiculous not really "walking" anywhere. Finally, after about 15 minutes, he came out the front door, and I was "coincidentally" walking Scruffy directly in front of the building in the flowerbed. When I saw him come out, I casually said, "Bye—nice to meet you!" He responded with a good-bye, and I was a little disappointed that there was nothing else mentioned. But then he turned around, came over to me, and asked, "I know this may sound odd, but would you like to get a drink sometime?" I was thrilled! I responded, "I'm glad you asked. Why do you think I've been pacing outside my apartment this entire time?" Verbal diarrhea strikes again. Then, he stammered, "Uh . . . um . . . well," so I jokingly said, "Now you ask for my number. I don't have my calendar on me since my phone is inside, so I can't check it to see when I'm free." I also mentioned to him what I do for a living. And we said our good-byes, this time for real.

By the time I got back into my apartment about five minutes later, I already had a very nice text message from him. We texted for about 20 more minutes, both with some witty banter and a confirmation of when we'd be going out (the following Monday), before I wrote, "Okay, some of us have to actually do work. ;) I'll talk to you later!" He said, "Ciao—talk to you later." That *should* have been the end of the conversation! Unfortunately, it wasn't.

About 10 minutes later, I received another text, this time with a picture. Uh oh. It was a shirtless selfie! Seriously?

And it said, "As a parting gift . . . lol" I didn't even know what to say! I just stared at my phone for a few minutes in utter disbelief. After a few hours, the time it took to muster up some semblance of a response, I wrote, "As both a nice girl and a dating coach, I have to tell you that sending a shirtless selfie is a major faux pas! Lucky you're cute." Wow.

Note to self (and all the men out there), no selfies, especially before the date!!!

Section 5

SEARCHING
AND EMAILING

In this section, you'll learn:

- How to properly search for potential matches
- How long to email one another before arranging a date
- What to say in a first online dating email
- How to transition from an "online" relationship to an "offline" date
- Which text messages are appropriate and which are not

Some people will inevitably love online dating, and some people will, of course, hate it. I'm clearly in the former category or else I wouldn't have started a business and written a book about it! This is what I always tell the skeptics: If you meet the love of your life online, you won't care how the heck you met—you'll just be thrilled that you did.

Everyone says, "Relationships take work," which is true. But finding love also takes work, which too few people realize. I wish we were all so lucky to have Prince Charming (or Princess Charming) fall into our arms over the frozen foods at the supermarket or end up in a seat next to us on a flight to Paris, but I don't know anyone who has that kind of luck. (Actually, I take that back. I do have a cousin who was lucky enough to have met his wife at the supermarket . . . and she didn't even speak English at the time!) Just like in our jobs, we have to make our own happiness, and I guess I would know since I quit my job in finance to follow this passion for helping people find love online. We have to do that in the love arena, too. Why not control your destiny a little? Maybe it won't make for the best story of how you met, but you won't care when you're in the arms of someone you love and who loves you back. Is it luck or persistence that leads to success at online dating? I'd venture to say a little bit of both.

Online dating isn't easy, which many people don't realize. They think they can just throw a profile up there and wait. No way, José. That's like walking into a bar and just plopping yourself on a stool without even trying to make conversation with anyone. Or, it's like signing up for the gym and assuming you'll lose weight simply because they charge your credit card some exorbitant fee on the 15th of every month. It's just not going to work. And I've realized that many people do not want to put in the effort, which is what led to my desire to start my business.

The naysayers, of course, always have something to say about online dating:

- "I can't write about myself." No problem! I hear there's a good book out there that can help you with this. Wink wink.
- "None of my pictures look good." You know there's a good smile in there somewhere! As we now know, less is more when it comes to pictures. A nice close-up smile goes a long way. And remember that taking professional photos is always an option if you have no recent photos.
- "But none of the people I like are writing to me." Who cares? You need to write to people also, which some people (especially women) find to be a novel concept. Why not take control over your contacts? I'll talk more about this later.
- "But what will I say?" Don't worry about it. Just write something short and sweet, taking into account both your personality and something from his or her profile.

It doesn't seem so bad anymore, does it? Yes—online dating takes work. But then again, so do most things in life that are worth the outcome. Trust me—it'll be worth it.

Chapter 15

THE SEARCH

I am still with [my girlfriend]. It has been 10 months now. I am extremely happy. You did a great job of getting me to my last first date!

—Jason, 38, Alexandria, VA

When searching for a potential mate, it's important to keep a few things in mind:

- **Update your search periodically to include new people.** Maybe Mr. or Ms. Right lives just five miles outside of your search radius.
- **Change how you sort your search occasionally.** One day, sort by newest members first, the next sort by activity date, the next perhaps sort by age. You may find some new people who fell to the bottom of your list before.
- **Try not to be too picky.** Will it really matter if someone is 5'8" versus 5'9" in the long run?

I could probably write a whole book on the topic of being too picky, but I'll spare you. I'm not so sure that would be a bestseller anyway!

Q&A with Erika

Q: If you were me, would you have gone out with some of the guys I decided not to contact?
—Deborah, 35, Washington, D.C.

A: It depends on the reason you didn't want to contact them. Complete lack of attraction—no need to email them. One thing in the profile that seemed iffy—why not? You have nothing to lose. I'm all about opening all the doors at the outset. You can always close them later if you want, but you might as well check someone out first before deciding.

Follow-up Q: And, did you find it was worth it to give people you're not sure about a chance? Like, was it encouraging or discouraging?

A: It's both. Sometimes you walk into the bar and see your date for the first time, and you're like, "There's just no way." That could be discouraging, of course. But they all make for great stories! Start writing down the really funny ones. I wish I had! I could have written a book.
Side note: And now here I am!

Q: I don't think the woman you set me up with next week is my type. You probably hear this a lot. Maybe you will be able to teach me to expand my perspectives and I can go with the flow a little more?
—Len, 46, Raleigh, NC

A: My philosophy is to open many possible doors (go on many dates) before you decide whether or not to close them, rather than closing doors before giving people a chance and getting to know them. You sometimes just don't know your "type" until you meet in person, and in my opinion, more dates are better than fewer dates. I actually liken it to clothes shopping for myself. I am very petite, so it's hard to find pants that fit. Rather than finding a pair I like and then being disappointed if it's not available in my size (only emailing women you like and then being disappointed if they don't respond), I search all of the clothes just to find my size and *then* decide if I like the pants (email and go out with more women and then decide who is right for you). It makes the pool larger, and it's all a numbers game.

Q: For me, I did not at all like the sound of him. There's one main reason—he admits he's had two significant relationships, yet he can offer no lessons learned. Nor can he delineate what he's looking for in a partner. To me, those show a lack of introspection. That's like not having any idea of what you're looking for professionally—and having no lessons learned from a series of jobs. Really? Either he's unreflective (which is definitely a non-negotiable for me) or he's emotionally closed off. I think my assumptions in the case above are reasonable. But if something seems glaringly unfair, I welcome your feedback.
—Elizabeth, 37, New York, NY

A: I think some of your assessments are fair, yet I also think you're reading into things too much. You can really only make these assessments after meeting with someone. For example, while I personally may write in a very jovial way, that doesn't mean I don't have an introspective side. It simply means my profile didn't show that side of me. I encourage my clients to keep the profile light and approachable, and perhaps he's doing the same. I'm not saying you have to like this guy, but I wouldn't put too much thought into analyzing every word of the profile.

EXTRA CHEESE, PLEASE

Someone once told me that online dating is like ordering a pizza. At first I laughed at that analogy, then I cringed, and then I realized he was right.

I'd like a large pie with extra cheese, mushrooms, sausage, and broccoli. But make sure the cheese is covering the whole pizza because I don't like baldness, and actually, why don't you hold the sausage? I'd like someone who doesn't eat processed meat. And while you're at it, make sure those mushrooms are well-educated, like maybe with an advanced degree of some sort. And as for the broccoli, can you make sure the stalks are a certain height because I only want tall broccoli. Could I get that to go? Thanks.

We are all looking for that on-paper perfect mate. And since online dating sites give so much choice in the matter, we think it's our right to have everything we're looking for. Now, I'm not saying there's anything wrong with wanting certain things, but what if someone out there looks promising but doesn't necessarily fit all of those objective criteria? What's a single person to do? My response is to give it a shot anyway.

When we walk into a bar or restaurant and see someone we like, that man or woman doesn't have a chart attached to his or her forehead full of credentials, stats, and dislikes. (Wouldn't that be a pretty funny sight, though?) We trust our instincts; we go with chemistry. But online, we have so much information that it's almost too easy to discard someone simply because he is 5'5" or she has a fondness for *US Weekly* rather than the latest issue of *The Economist*. (I'm not saying I know anyone like that, of course!)

I was chatting with someone a few years ago who met her boyfriend at a rock climbing wall. They had known each other for a while, and ironically enough, when they eventually started dating, he came up as one of her suggested matches on OkCupid that week. She looked at his profile and said, "I would have never gone out with him after reading this." I guess she thought she was in the mood for a pizza with the works, but in reality, what she wanted was much simpler—plain cheese.

So, go ahead, order whatever you want for dinner tonight, but when it comes to dating, there's no check-box order to place. Give people the benefit of the doubt, because in the end, after meeting in person, chemistry may trump all to give you the slice of your life.

ALL MEN GO BALD . . .
AND HAVE EARWAX

Then there's the advice I got from my dad many years ago when he thought I was being too picky about the men I would (or wouldn't) date. He doesn't give much advice in the love department (he and my mom have been married for almost 35 years), but this piece of advice was a rare gem. I once told my parents in passing that I didn't care for bald men. Oy—that was a huge mistake. (My dad is bald, as were both my grandpas.)

As I said, my dad rarely gives me love advice, but one day as I was going through my voicemails, I came across this one from my dad: "Hi Eri. I love you. Don't forget that all men go bald, okay? And you know what else? All men have earwax." Then he said, "So go out with them." Keep in mind that my dad jokes around a lot, so he was just being silly about the earwax part, but maybe what he was saying actually had some truth to it. Was he right? If you like someone, you may be able to overlook things that you would normally not go for, online or otherwise. I remember I once met a guy (at jury duty, of all places) whom I really liked for his effervescent personality, and because of that, I actually thought his bald spot was kind of cute. But then I thought to myself, would I have given him a chance if I had seen him online? Maybe not.

We are very good (women especially, but also men) at speculating about a person or ruling him or her out based on one small thing—I don't like blondes, he picked a terrible spot for our date, he has a tattoo, she wore an ugly shirt—but who cares? Does the bar where you meet or an ugly shirt really matter in life? Nope. Is this person nice, genuine, and thoughtful? Those are the things that matter. You might go on many more bad dates by being more open-minded about the people you choose, but it makes the pool of potentials that much larger.

On a related note, we also often talk ourselves out of things because of one little hang-up. He works here, so he must be this way, so I won't like him, so I won't email him. Sound familiar? I actually sometimes think of it as a job search. About six years ago, while I was still working at Fannie Mae, I found a job within the company that happened to be located in California. I really wanted to apply for it. I used to think that I would one day move to California to be a movie star. (A girl can dream, right?) At any rate, I almost didn't apply for the job because of the fact that I might have to turn it down in the end if I decided not to move. But then I thought to myself—why not give myself the chance to think about it and then turn it down *after* I get the job? So, I applied. I didn't get it anyway, but I was glad I gave myself the chance. It's the same thing with the online dating game: It's best to give yourself the chance to turn something down if, in the end, it's not what you want. But you might as well open more doors at the outset, because maybe hiding behind that one thing that doesn't seem perfect is a great person.

So, try to forget for a minute that he's bald . . . or has earwax. Thanks, Dad.

RIDICULOUS DEAL-BREAKERS

Like I said, I could go on all day about being too picky, but I'll just add one last thought on this subject. I can't say I love *The Millionaire Matchmaker* Patti Stanger's advice on everything (and I certainly don't try to emulate her rather harsh demeanor), but once in a while she shares a nugget of information that I can get behind. This time it has to do with non-negotiables and deal-breakers. Stanger tells her clients to limit their non-negotiables to five things that they either can't live with or can't live without.[3] I don't know if five is the magic number, or if there is a magic number at all, but having a long laundry list of a dozen "must haves" will inevitably doom your search for Mr. or Ms. Perfect. In reality, no one is perfect, so it's important to know what you are willing to bend on.

I hear them all: *I don't want a guy under 5'11". She must weigh less than 120 pounds. If he owns a cat, forget about it. If she likes to play board games, she must be a nerd. He puts Splenda in his coffee—that's so passé. She's never been outside the United States, so she must not have any idea about other cultures. I can't go out with him if he has the dry cleaner crease in his shirt. She's older than I am by a month, and I refuse to date an older woman. He does this weird thing where he wiggles one ear when he's nervous.* The list goes on and on.

What's really important in life? I always had two main non-negotiables: intelligence and religion. I knew that I wanted someone to be smart—really smart. Not that I'm Einstein or anything, but I have dated people who weren't as intellectually stimulating as I wanted, and it bothered me. As for religion, I am Jewish. I'm not terribly religious (mmm . . . bacon), and I'm more culturally Jewish than anything else (I make a heck of a matzah ball soup), but it was the common background that I craved. Nothing else seemed as important except for some age boundaries and physical attraction. And the latter is so hard to sense until you meet in person.

In the end, what's most important is how someone treats you. So think about the few things that really matter to you and stick to those. Beyond that, throw caution to the wind and date lots of different types of people until you find that one who makes you happy, whether he has a crease in his shirt or not.

Chapter 16

EMAIL ETIQUETTE

ERIKA! This is so good!! I love it, you hit a homerun here. I really feel you captured my personality and expressed so many things people wouldn't usually "get" unless they had met/knew me somehow. There is definitely some genius behind your technique . . . WOW, Erika—it's only been 12 hours since I sent out those emails and we're already at 40 percent for responses. PLUS emails from other random people we didn't contact. You're goooooooood!

—Rob, 34, Philadelphia, PA

In almost every aspect of life, we go after the things we want. Not happy in a job? Search for a new one. Some recent weight gain getting you down? Up the ante during your workouts. Why is it, then, that in dating, we think happiness will just find us? It's as if we think we have a sign on our foreheads flashing, "Single and ready to mingle." A client recently emailed me about a guy who, unfortunately, didn't work out in the relationship department. She wrote, "I just wanted the easy route, which was a guy who liked me to show up and be perfect, but I guess that has kind of a fairy tale ring to it. Oh well." Sadly, as she's starting to realize, that's just not how it works. In online dating, writing a great profile is only half the battle. To really be successful, you have to be proactive and email people of interest.

Now that you've found some potential matches using the advice in the previous chapters, it's time to send some emails. And women, it's important for you to email potential matches, too. Many women think that emailing a potential mate might make them seem less feminine or lose the upper hand at the get-go. This just isn't true. Again, we need to go for what we want in life, and it starts here. Also, many people may not be as open-minded as you are, and their search criteria might not catch you. For example, maybe you're looking within a 20-mile radius of your zip code, but your potential match is looking within 10 miles. Unless you email first, the other person won't know you exist. So if you don't send the first email, that perfect match may never find you.

As for what to include in the email, it's actually pretty simple:

1. Something about his or her profile that caught your attention
2. Something about you and how it relates to him or her
3. A question to end the email

In terms of length, just a few sentences can get the ball rolling. No one wants to read a novel-length email after a long day of work. And no form letters! It's very clear when people copy and paste the same email from person to person. That's a surefire way to get zero responses. Someone actually told me the other day that both she and her roommate received the *same exact* email from a guy on OkCupid. Email fail. Now that we know the rules, let's look at several sample emails that work:

Welcome to the area! Where were you before moving here? I actually moved here from the West Coast myself, so I think I have the best of the two worlds—a taste for both good wine and historical monuments.

Since you mentioned you like music but don't know much about it, I can help you with the difference between a note and a chord if you'll tell me something about aeronautics and space. What exactly do you do in the field?

Looking forward to hearing from you,

Suzy

♥ ♥ ♥

And I thought I had a lot of degrees! Congratulations on getting your PhD. What's next? A Nobel Prize? Haha. I really appreciate when people value education as much as I do. I actually got my PhD in physics before moving here three months ago.

Now for the fun stuff . . . it looks like we both love food. I just went to Graffiato the other day, and I liked it a lot. Do you have a #1 place that I have to try here?

Cheers,

John

♥ ♥ ♥

You grew up in LA, and I decided to come out to LA for college. We're like two ships passing in the night. I also went to China for a year, so there's really no method to my madness. But I've definitely had some incredible experiences along the way . . . and amazing food.

I'm disappointed you don't have any pictures of your dog, by the way! I'm definitely a sucker for all furry creatures. What kind of dog is it?

Best,

Melanie

♥ ♥ ♥

As I read your profile, I was especially curious to hear about your former career in music. How did you get into that, and do you ever miss it? I can't say I'm terribly musical myself (no one would pay to hear me . . . in fact, they may pay not to!), but I do enjoy listening to Pandora while I'm at the gym. Have you been to any good concerts in the area recently?

Looking forward to hearing from you,

Larry

♥ ♥ ♥

I have to ask about your line, "Love women who love words." Are we talking women with a big vocabulary? Just curious. Regardless, I like words. In fact, I use them daily.

Since you seem to be into good food as much as I am (not a small feat), what are some of your favorite restaurants in the area?

Yolanda

♥ ♥ ♥

You're a golfer. I'm miserable at golf. Are we doomed from the start? ;) I do like your philosophy, though, of treating every day like a holiday. If only that meant we could take off work every day.

Have you been in Atlanta the whole time (I noticed you grew up here), or did you leave for a bit and move back? I'm originally from this area, but I went to school in St. Louis and Philly before coming back home. Something about this area (perhaps family guilt?) makes everyone come back!

Michelle

In the end, you can't win the lottery unless you play, so you might as well try your hand at the lottery of love to see what it has in store. Now, go forth and email!

MORE EMAIL ETIQUETTE (ADVICE FOR MEN)

Hey baby!

Hey, beautiful.

What's up, hot stuff?

You must be tired because you've been running around my mind all day!

If you've ever sent someone an email like the ones above, then you know the outcome: crickets. No respectable woman (assuming that's what you're looking for) wants to receive an email that not only shows that you didn't read her profile but also turns her into a piece of meat rather than acknowledging the real person that she is. I made up the lines above, but below are **real, unedited emails** that female clients of mine have received on various online dating sites that were appalling and certainly not the right way to get someone to respond favorably:

Your profile caught my eye and I am a little embarrassed to tell you why. You look just like . . . You look like the mom next door, but I can't help but think you're super naughty. It is really hot. You are innocent and sweet looking, but it is like you are thinking something less than pure in your head. I don't know why I got that feel, but I did. It just makes me think you are very sexy milf! haha Okk, sorry! That was too forward! hah

♥ ♥ ♥

Wow ok . . . So u probably get alot of bull crap messages so I'm just going to be real. I would like to know u and take u out lol. U wanna know more about me, write me :-) hope to hear from soon

♥ ♥ ♥

Shut up and let me take u out

♥ ♥ ♥

Too bad for me that I am married!!!!

♥ ♥ ♥

Hello there, you're very pretty! I wish you were my girlfriend!

These are bad, and I hope I don't have to explain why. Now that we've gotten what *not* to do out of the way, let's look at the top five creative ways to get women to message you back:

1. **Speak like a human.**

   Okay, this one admittedly isn't very creative, but it is necessary. Please check for grammar and punctuation . . . and don't use "text speak." If you want to say "you," then write it out rather than using "u" instead. It'll go further than you may think.

2. **Make sure she knows you read her profile.**

   This is another fairly boring tip, I know, but it's important that you don't just comment on her "foxy figure." Rather, comment on how she completely beat your time in the marathon or how impressive it is that she actually practiced the piano when she was little, unlike someone you know who looks oddly like you.

3. **Use a quirky or creative subject line.**

   Would you rather answer an email with "Enjoyed your profile" or "Alien invasion—take cover" as the subject line? Unless you're actually concerned about aliens (or don't like people with a sense of humor), then I'm guessing you'd choose the latter. So will she. Another fun one I saw recently read, "Tell your boss to give you a raise," written to a woman who was self-employed.

4. **Always end your email with a question, preferably a relevant and fun one.**

   Not fun: "How are you enjoying the weather these days?" (Seriously? Are we already resorting to conversations about the weather?)

   Fun: "So your friends say you're loyal, funny, and adventurous . . . that's great! But what I want to know is this: How would your enemies describe you? ;-)" This email even makes great use of someone's inevitable empty adjectives.

   Another fun one: "I love the fact that chocolate chip cookies were listed as the first thing on your 'can't live without' list. Now, I have a very important question for you: With walnuts or without?"

And the most effective . . .

5. **Tease her in a way that makes her want to tease you back.**

   "I see that you're a Red Sox fan. Hmm . . . that doesn't bode well for us considering I love my Yankees. It's a good thing you also mentioned that you like an IPA and Scotch. Redeemed!"

   Another example: "You dislike sushi? Okay, I'm going to have to work on that one with you. We won't start out with eel or anything raw. Deal?"

Obviously, no one can ever guarantee that your email will receive a response, but if you follow these tips rather than your usual "What's up?" email, then you're at least off to a good start into online dating bliss.

Q&A with Erika

Q: Some of the emails are obvious that I will not be answering, but I'm wondering what I should do about winks and the emails that are not so obvious what to do with. For example, several guys wrote something to the effect of, "You seem interesting. Write me." How do you recommend that I handle those?
—Allyson, 41, Washington, D.C.

A: To answer your question, for the ones who either wink or write short messages, it's up to you whether to write/respond after reading their profiles. If they sound appealing, it can't hurt. On the one hand, maybe they are just lazy by doing that, and on the other, maybe they're clueless as to how this thing works, too. The good ones will send (or respond with) an email showing that they at least read some part of your profile.

Chapter 17

MUCH MORE EMAIL ETIQUETTE

People join online dating sites for many reasons: to find an activity partner, a fling, a friend, a date, a long-term relationship, marriage, or marriage and children. Some online dating sites are even nice enough to lay out all of these choices side-by-side for us. All it takes is the click of a button or two to list what we'd like to find in our online dating adventure. Curiously enough, "pen pal" is not an option. In fact, nothing of the sort is listed—not "letter-writer," "someone to keep me occupied at work," or "email buddy." Nope—it's just not a choice. Why? Because people do not join online dating sites simply to email back and forth. **People are looking to form a relationship, not an e-lationship.**

The scenario always starts out the same. We find someone good-looking who fits the bulk of our criteria. We send a short and sweet email out into the ether just hoping for a response . . . and to our delight, we get one. (Remember, as we discussed before, both men and women should be emailing people of interest.) We write a witty response back, spell checking twice, sweating a little bit, and editing a little more. Finally, we send it off, waiting the requisite few hours or even a day just to make sure it doesn't look like we've been sitting by our computer twiddling our thumbs (even if we have). Sometimes we get nothing back again (so annoying), and sometimes we do . . . time to celebrate! So, we email back, sharing information about ourselves, our jobs, and our lives outside of the confines of online dating. And, much to our delight again, we keep getting responses. But response after response, nothing seems to lead to a date request.

When it comes to online dating, the best way to play your cards is to ask someone out after just a few emails back and forth. Chemistry, which I call the "wild card," is impossible to gauge over email, so a few extra emails won't make or break it. The best way to see if there's any spark is to meet in person, and the sooner the better. If you plan the first date quickly and like each other, that's great—you'll have more time to spend together! If you don't have that connection, you can move on more quickly without investing too much of your time. In fact, I don't even recommend talking on the phone before a date. Someone might be great on the phone and a dud in person, or a bore on the phone and fabulous in person. The point is that you never know whether you'll have chemistry until you actually meet, and no number of emails will change that.

For men, it's not too forward to ask someone out for a drink or coffee (no dinner, which we'll discuss later) after one or two emails. If a woman responds to your email or reaches out to you on her own, she's probably interested enough to meet in person. She'll likely get a bit restless after about the fourth or fifth email with no date in sight, so it's best to lock in the date before that happens. Emails are nice, but in the end, we're looking for something real, someone real, and not just some words on a page, or an e-lationship.

It's also important to respond in a timely fashion, as you would with a friend or a coworker. What would be considered a timely fashion, anyway? Anything from a few hours to two days would be considered appropriate. Responding to someone's email too quickly may imply that you have nothing better to do (even if that's not the case at all), and taking too long to respond implies that you're not interested. Obviously there are exceptions to every rule, such as if someone is on vacation or has an abnormally busy week at work, but generally speaking, a prompt (but not too prompt) response will serve you well.

Now that we've discussed responding to someone of interest in a timely fashion, what happens if you are not interested in someone who reaches out to you? Unfortunately, while pretty darn rude, the general rule of thumb is not to respond to the email at all. I actually have major pet peeves about people not responding to my emails in general. Am I not a person? Am I not important enough for you? Are you "too busy" to make time for even a one-word response to acknowledge that I exist? (You get the point.) But when it comes to online dating, radio silence is the way of showing a lack of interest. Sometimes, though, the note is so thoughtful that, while you're still not interested, you do want to at least acknowledge that you appreciated the thought. In this case, it's really up to you whether to respond or not. You can simply do nothing (again, I know it sounds horrible, and it took me a long time to embrace this concept), or you can thank the person for his or her time and say that, while you appreciated the thoughtful note, you don't think the two of you are a match. The potential downfall of being nice, however, is that the person may then ask you why you feel that way, or worse, berate you for not giving him or her a chance, which could lead to a pretty awkward email exchange. As they say, no good deed goes unpunished. So proceed with caution.

Now, let's get back to the people we like. You're sending emails back and forth, being flirtatious, and then all of a sudden your potential new mate stops emailing you out of the blue, or as I like to call this phenomenon, "drops off the earth." It's disconcerting, isn't it? You read and reread your emails to see if you said something offensive. You pore over your pictures to see if there was something that turned this person off. You have no idea what the heck happened! Just remember this: It's not you. People fall off the earth for many reasons—they started seeing someone else, they lost interest, they got busy, etc. You cannot put the blame on yourself. But it doesn't feel good, does it? For this reason, I implore you not to fall off the earth for someone else. Instead, send a quick note saying that you won't be following up. Perhaps it's something like, "It's been great getting to know you, but I started seeing someone else, and I want to see where it goes," or "In reading your profile again, I'm just not sure we're the right fit, but I wish you the best of luck." Honesty (or mostly honesty) is the best policy in this case, especially if you've sent more than three emails back and forth (which is more than I'd even recommend anyway).

Sometimes, even if you are interested in someone and you have the date scheduled, something comes up, causing you or your date to cancel. It happens. But, if it does happen, please make sure to call your date rather than texting, or worse, emailing over the online dating site. We have no idea whether the other person has access to his or her email during the day or even his or her phone, for that matter. Don't let common courtesy go out the window—make the call. On that note, if the person cancelling does not offer an alternative date, he or she may have decided not to go through with the date for one reason or another. Again, don't blame yourself. It could be cold feet, it could be a last-minute second-guessing of things, or it could be no reason at all. If you do need to cancel and still want to meet the other person at some point, please do suggest an alternate date immediately, or he or she will assume you're not interested, even if that's not the case. It's a small world out there, so it's best to treat everyone with respect, even if you've never met, because you may run into them tomorrow.

How will you call, though, if you don't have your date's number? I recommend exchanging phone numbers a day or two before the date for this reason alone. You want to be able to contact each other if some unforeseen circumstance comes up, or even if you're just running late.

Lastly, when you email people, many will simply not respond. Back in 2009, OkCupid's blog (*OkTrends*) came out with a study saying that the average response rate on its site was 32 percent.[4] Keep in mind that at that time, the average age on the site was 24, so feel free to take these results with a grain of salt if you're older than that, which I assume most of my readers are. The point here is to remember not to take it personally if someone you wrote to doesn't respond. It happens to the best of us.

For a fun aside, I'll share with you that I'm not only an online dating coach, but I'm also a singer and actress. And this line is what I say when I don't get the part: **They must not have liked my hair.** Their loss!

What does this have to do with dating? When we put ourselves out there by sending people emails on an online dating site, we risk the chance of not getting an email back. Let me be clear: Non-response does not equal rejection. In other words, the absence of a positive reply (an email back) is not the same as someone turning you down.

There's good reason not to treat the lack of a response as a rejection. Who knows why people don't respond? The *why* isn't the important part because it's often out of our control. Maybe you look like an ex, maybe he dismissed you for having one silly typo (remember to proofread!), maybe she had a business trip and didn't get to check her online dating account recently. Whatever the reason, just chalk it up to "They must not have liked my hair."

True, the lack of response makes it that much harder to deal with when you fall in love with someone's profile and think you're destined to be together, right? A former client of mine whom we'll call Robbie came across a woman online who was also a marathon-runner, loved cookie dough ice cream, and thought that doing the *New York Times* crossword puzzle was the best thing since sliced bread. He was obsessed with her profile and asked me to help him craft an email to win her over. I did. But I warned him that should she not respond, they weren't meant to be, and that was that. He'd likely find a butter pecan–loving woman who much preferred Sudoku, and they'd be just as compatible because she'd expand his horizons. Until someone responds, he or she can't be the love of your life . . . and for poor Robbie, she wasn't. You're lusting over some words and a picture on a screen. It's only when you get a response that the person becomes real. For that reason, I recommend sending emails to more people than you're inclined to, because ultimately, it's a numbers game. The more emails you send, the more responses you get. 32 percent of 20 is more than 32 percent of 10, right? (You don't have to be a math genius to know that one!) And who doesn't want responses?

You may be asking, "Are you telling me to email people I'm just 'meh' about in order to get a response?" Sort of, yes. As we all know, many of us present ourselves better in person than we do on screen, so if you're even somewhat interested in a person's online dating profile, go for the email. As you know by now, I'm a fan of opening all possible doors, or sending emails, and then closing them later (after some emailing back and forth or after a date) if the person is ultimately not what you want. But in the end, the right ones will respond because you each see something promising in the other. As my dad used to say (his second piece of love advice, as if the earwax wasn't enough!), it's all about receptivity. Someone needs to be receptive to what *you* have to offer, and in turn, you need to be receptive to what *he or she* has to offer. Otherwise, it just won't work.

So, feel free to send those emails. What's the worst that could happen—you don't get a response? No biggie. They just didn't like your hair.

Q&A with Erika

Q: A problem I am currently having is the "date follow-through." Guys will ask me out on a date on-line, usually saying something like, "Let's get drinks next week." I say something like, "That sounds great. I'm free on Tuesday and Thursday after work around 6:30." Then sometimes, they don't get back to me. Or (in the case of the one guy I had a great date with) he said, "Let's hang out this week." I gave him my schedule in the same way as above. Then he told me that he's busy this week. I said, "Maybe the weekend." It's now two days later and there's no response.

I think that I might be too forward with guys. I'm a very forward and direct person in general and have to make sure that I limit this trait because guys want to be in control. When guys casually ask me out on a

date online, is there a better way to make it happen without scaring them off by being too forward?
—Carly, 23, Boston, MA

A: You actually remind me of myself in terms of being forward and being a planner, and there is nothing wrong with that—it's just your personality. (And it's not like you're asking the men out!) Doesn't it annoy you when a guy doesn't follow through or drops the ball? Well, if it annoys you now after one date or even before the date, it'll annoy you throughout life. So, rather than changing your tactic (giving two choices, like Tuesday or Thursday, as you said, is what I would recommend as well because it tells him when you're free but ultimately lets him pick the final date), it's more about finding a mature guy who actually takes the lead and doesn't just casually ask you out with no intention of putting something on the calendar. If you do want to soften it a little, you could say, "That sounds great. Tuesday or Thursday might work for me if that works for you." It's a little less forward and more "cool" with the word "might" in there and the time (after 6:30) removed. In short, you're doing nothing wrong here by being a planner. You'll likely end up with a fellow planner who is able to actually look at his calendar and commit to a date.

Q: So I'm relearning the etiquette of this thing and I just wanted to know whether it is okay if after like a three-time email exchange if I (the girl) can suggest

meeting? I just hate the email exchanges—I feel like I'm wasting my time if we have no chemistry.
—Jennie, 26, Washington, D.C.

A: To answer your question, it is more than okay after two or three emails to suggest meeting. Don't let him try to have an e-lationship with you. A good way to do it is to say, "Hey—I'm enjoying these emails. Should we meet up sometime next week for a drink? I'm free _____ or _____ if either works for you." That way, it's not quite as forward, and you're giving him choices, so he still feels like he gets to choose the final date. Works like a charm.

Q: So I asked this girl out who wrote me back, and I gave her a five-day advance notice of when I wanted to go out. I didn't hear back. So I "nudged" her (I'm going to patent that, by the way!) with a follow-up a couple of days later, and this is what I got back later that day: "I am sorry, but I can't meet you this week. I just started a new position last week, and I am working very long hours. Maybe another time." Obviously she's not interested, so why even write me at all? My take is that it doesn't matter—if she's not interested then she's not interested, so I keep moving on.
—Jonah, 35, Richmond, VA

A: From the response she sent, you're more than likely correct that she currently has no interest, whether she did or not when she wrote back to you. (Sorry!) She would have suggested another time to meet if she really wanted to. I have no idea why she'd bother responding in the first place if she was never interested. It's not even a good excuse, if you ask me. On the off-chance that she really is overwhelmed with work (happens to the best of us), you could try arranging something one more time, but I wouldn't be surprised if she declines. It has nothing to do with you. I like that you used the "soft ask," like I suggested. Even "I hope I'm not being too forward" before you ask her out goes a long way with certain people. That's why everyone's on these sites anyway—to go on dates—so it's never really too forward to ask someone out early. Onward! And for the record, I have a trademark on "A Little Nudge." Beat you to it!

Q: Hi, Erika. I am so disappointed that I am not sure what to think. My date had my phone number . . . why didn't he call to cancel? Had you not checked my Match account and caught me to tell me that he cancelled before we were scheduled to meet, I would have sat there feeling horribly stood up. Am I being too silly, touchy, or am I overreacting? Please advise.
—Leslie, 55, Rockville, MD

A: I am 100% in agreement with you. As I said on the phone, it's a huge red flag that your date did not call. I checked the time, and he emailed you at 5:02 p.m. saying that he couldn't make it. What's to think that you wouldn't have been out all day and just planned on meeting him at 7:00 without checking your Match.com email? He should have called, and that's that. I'm just glad I checked.

He can suggest another date if he wants. If he does try to reschedule, perhaps it's best to politely say in the next email that calling would have been more appropriate if he wasn't going to make it.

Q: It's been my experience that women sometimes read into things that men simply don't. For example, if a guy sends an intro email at 2:30 a.m., it may be perceived in a negative context . . . something along the lines of, "What is this idiot doing up at 2:30 on a Tuesday?" Is there a good, or should I say, politically correct, time to be sending these things?
—Russell, 37, San Francisco, CA

A: It's true—people (although, it's both men and women) read into things that we shouldn't sometimes. I'd try to email back at night, probably before midnight, to make things look a little more "normal." But if that stops a woman from responding, that's just silly.

Q: I had someone go quiet after she wrote to me and I wrote her back, and I'm trying to think if there is a way to get the dialogue started again. This has happened a few times. Please let me know if you have any ideas.
—Cameron, 42, Alexandria, VA

A: To start off broadly, I have both male and female clients in equal numbers telling me about the "disappearing act" that people are prone to do online. I'll tell you that when someone really likes you and wants to get to know you, she won't go anywhere. That said, she was interested enough to reach out the first time, so it doesn't hurt to "nudge" her a bit. I would make your next note funny, though. Perhaps write something like, "I just wanted to check in and make sure you weren't trapped under a rock somewhere or eaten by a seal. (Side note: Where do I come up with this stuff?) Assuming my last email just got buried somehow, I wanted to quickly check in to say hi because I'm still interested in getting to know you." Or, you could simply email her saying, "I hope your week is going well." This may also get the ball rolling again. Then, it's out of your control. Also, I would try to make a point of asking a woman out very early on in the process. For example, if you write and she answers, it's perfectly okay to ask her out in the next email.

Chapter 18

GETTING TO THE DATE

So, check this out. A woman emails me and gets right to the point that she wants to go out for coffee. She seemed very nice, but the problem was that her photo was such that I couldn't really tell what she looked like. Finally, I decide to just roll with your advice, meet her in person, and evaluate things face to face. She rolls into Starbucks right on time. My jaw hits the floor. Oh my god . . . absolutely drop-dead gorgeous! I was just stunned. Instant chemistry, two hour coffee, second date lined up. The entire time I'm thinking, this can't be happening. If Erika were here, she'd be laughing hysterically with an "I told you so." Too funny.

—Lance, 53, Silver Spring, MD

Now that we've discussed creating the perfect profile and emailing people who strike our fancy, there's one last step: Getting to the date! Unfortunately for many, getting to the actual in-person, face-to-face date is easier said than done. Why? People have a tendency to get in their own way.

We all know what an obstacle is. According to good ol' *Merriam-Webster*, an obstacle is "something that impedes progress or achievement." Now, what if that "something" is you?

In dating, there are so many potential obstacles to that first date:

1. Emailing someone online for too long
2. Talking on the phone before the date (I don't recommend this, which I'll further explain in a minute.)
3. Text messaging before the date

Each of the obstacles listed above is a potential **rejection point** for your date to decide not to go out with you (and vice versa). Now, I know I'm a former economist and all, but you don't need to be a math whiz to know that by removing one of these potential rejection points, your chances of getting to the date are greater.

Let's look at a few scenarios below:

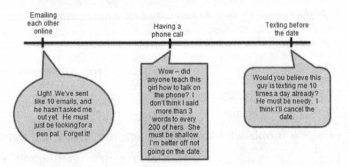

At each point, the date is presumed to have messed up in some way, but there may be an explanation for all of it. For Endless Emailer Eddie, perhaps he just doesn't know how online dating works. Give him the benefit of the doubt and (gasp!) even suggest meeting him. For Chatty Cathy on the phone, perhaps she just gets nervous and talks too much, but as she gets to know you, she'll calm down a bit and actually breathe between talking about her precious pet cockatoo and her trip to Iceland last year. As I mentioned earlier, someone might be terrible on the phone and great in person, or great on the phone and not as great in the flesh. The reason I do not recommend talking on the phone before a first online date is because it's too easy to judge someone based on his or her voice or lack of phone skills. It's much better to find out how this person behaves in real life. I have a pretty nasal voice myself, and I certainly don't want to be judged for it! For Texting Tommy, maybe he's just excited to go out with a great catch like you. It's better than the alternative—not contacting you at all. Simply saying, "I'm not really a huge texter" should do the trick and stop him from the excessive pre-date texting.

Do Eddie, Cathy, and Tommy hit a bit close to home? Or maybe you've dismissed one of them in your dating days. My advice? Remove the obstacles to the first date. You never know if you'll have chemistry until you meet in person, so don't get in your own way by setting up all of these rejection points. A couple of emails back and forth should do the trick, and then get right to the date. A client recently emailed me saying, "What came across in emails was not there in person. I guess that happens quite a bit and the more experience I get at this, the sooner I will try to get to a meeting so I don't have to [spend] my time emailing." Obviously, this can go either way—better in person or worse—but you have to actually meet to find out.

Q&A with Erika

Q: Just curious . . . in email correspondence back and forth, at what point is it appropriate to ask for a number? When is it an appropriate time to call her? —Douglas, 33, Charlotte, NC

A: If she answers your email, ask her out in the next email. Nix the phone call—just plan the date. Only exchange numbers at the end in case someone is running late. Especially in the younger generations, for better or for worse, people aren't talking on the phone as much anyway.

Q: So I have a question for you about some of the guys who are contacting me online. I get it. Guys want to get to the date as quickly as possible. But I get a lot of guys who just ask me out in that first email, without much other chatting. I'm totally on board with getting to the date as soon as possible, but I need a little interaction beforehand, be it on the phone or email, to assure me that we've got some kind of basic rapport. And frankly, if I said yes to all of them, I wouldn't have any time left! So is there some way that I can encourage these guys to chat a little beforehand (because some of them do seem interesting)? I've tried asking them to call me (under

the guise of setting up the date) or emailing them back with questions, but they just disappear.
—Emily, 36, Seattle, WA

A: You ask a good question. People have short attention spans when it comes to online dating, so while this may not be what you want to hear, I'd accept the offer from those who interest you, simply based on their profile and the one email. This is a much better "problem" than what usually happens—the e-lationship. If you try to maintain a back-and-forth correspondence, the guy may think you're looking for a pen pal or are simply not that interested, so he gives up. I'd use your discretion, based on his profile, pictures, and that first email, to decide whether to go on the date or not. And remember, a "date" is only going to be coffee or a drink, so you'll have an excuse to leave after the one drink if need be. Lastly, I don't recommend talking on the phone before the first date. It's too hard to gauge chemistry that way, so meeting in person first is generally the best option.

A NOTE ON TEXT MESSAGING, OR TEXTIQUETTE, BEFORE THE FIRST DATE:

Like I just mentioned, for better or for worse, the days of calling a woman and asking her out are slowly becoming a thing of the past. (If you are one of the men who still calls, then I have a lot of respect for you.) A phone call is still the best method for asking a woman out if you've met her in person already or a friend is fixing you up. If you met online, as you know, I recommend just scheduling the date over email, sans the call.

Texting, of course, has its advantages: Rejection seems less painful, you can do it anytime and anywhere (even from the comfort of your own bed . . . or bathroom), and it doesn't take as much courage to ask someone out. If you should decide that you're not going to buck up and make the call, then the text should be clear, concise, and, most importantly, nice. In addition, it's best to confirm (generally done by the gentleman) a day before the date. Saying something like, "Really looking forward to seeing you tomorrow at 7:00" should work wonders. Your date will be thrilled to see that you're on the ball. As a side note, in that confirmation, take the confident approach I just mentioned rather than meekly asking, "Are we still on for tomorrow?" Confidence is sexy.

Texting is also great if you're running late, can't find parking, or can't find your date for some reason. Let's just hope it's not because his or her profile pictures were from 15 years ago!

What not to do at this stage: cancel via text on the day of the date. If you have your date's phone number, please have the courtesy to call. This goes for both men and women.

Section 6

SAFETY FIRST

In this section, you'll learn:

- What red flags to look for in a profile
- Which emails to avoid and which to pay close attention to
- How to protect yourself and stay safe when online dating

Chapter 19

RED FLAGS

People ask me all the time what "red flags" to look for when reading someone's online dating profile or emails. Obviously, much of what you determine to be a red flag will be subjective, just like your deal-breakers, but it's important to keep an eye out for a few things:

- **Photos with dates from more than two or three years ago . . . or no pictures at all**

  This person may be trying to deceive you into thinking that he or she looks like a younger, and often more attractive, version of himself or herself. Or, by not posting any pictures, again, he or she may be hiding something from you.

- **Too many pictures not showing the profile-writer's face**

  Whether it's true or not, it looks like he or she is trying to hide something.

- **A litany of things the person doesn't want in a partner instead of what he or she does want**

  We already discussed positive versus negative. If the person is listing many negative things, it's possible that he or she is bitter for some reason or might be just out of a relationship and is simply rehashing all of the negative qualities in the last partner.

- **Contradictory information**

  If you find information in someone's profile that seems to contradict itself, such as age, occupation, number of children, marital status, or level of education, it may be a lie that is not so well disguised.

- **A novel-esque email to you that says nothing about your profile but goes on to tell his or her life story**

  This is a copy/paste job at its finest. If the person is still of interest to you, I would recommend responding with, "I'd love to hear what piqued your interest about my profile." Then you'll either get a real, personalized response or you won't.

- **A first email with his or her email address and phone number in it**

  Something just screams "fishy" here. Why the urgency?

- **An email containing strange links to photos or third-party websites**

  Creepy. Enough said. And potentially a lurking computer virus. Don't click!

- **An email asking for any personal information besides your phone number or email address, such as social security number, date of birth, address, or even bank account number**

If any of this happens, run. And run fast! I would also block this user and alert the online dating company as you see fit.

- **A lack of commitment to meet in person, either by dodging the question or cancelling several times**
  There is probably a reason that he or she is not agreeing to meet. It's time to correspond with someone who is excited at the prospect of meeting in person. This leads me to the topic of "catfishing," which means that someone is pretending to be someone else to lure in potential dates or romantic interests.

When people hear the term "online dating," they don't always know what it means. Here's what it definitely does not mean:

- Having a virtual girlfriend or boyfriend
- Dating in your pajamas for the rest of eternity while eating a pint of Chunky Monkey
- Sitting behind your computer and assuming that you just had a "date"

In many ways, "online dating" could be considered a misnomer. It could instead be called something like "online introductions" because the actual dating part should still be in person. Period.

It's easy to fall in love with someone's online persona, isn't it? Wow—she and I both love Maroon 5! She and I both just ran our first marathon—we're meant to be together! She looks just like Rachel McAdams—I'm in love! But remember that this person is not real until you've had a face-to-face inter-action. It's just words on a page and a picture until then. We already discussed avoiding the e-lationship and poor Robbie's disappointment when his "love" didn't respond to him. I'll simply reiterate it here.

As mentioned before, it is generally not too forward to ask someone out for a drink or coffee after one or two emails back and forth. If a woman responds to your email or reaches out to you on her own, she's probably interested enough to meet in person. But if she keeps dodging your efforts to meet, and she has no plausible explanation, then perhaps she's not who she says she is (or is just not that interested).

Let's say you ask a woman out, and she says she's busy. Okay, you can look past that this time around. Now, you ask her out again, and she's busy again. Either she's secretly the President of the Universe, or she is trying to get out of meet-ing for some reason. The best thing you can do is to ask *her* to suggest a time to meet that works for her. That way, the ball is in her court. If she dodges again, then it's time to move on to someone who wants to meet you in real life.

If meeting in person is not feasible for some reason (per-haps you don't live close enough to meet in a timely fash-ion), then the best thing to do is to suggest that you Skype or FaceTime. It takes just as long to dial someone's phone number and chat for a few minutes as it does to sit down and email each other, so if someone declines this offer, that is a major red flag.

My advice? Meet offline as soon as you can. If you like each other, you'll be glad you didn't waste all that time emailing. And if you don't, you can move on and also be glad you didn't waste all that time emailing. Win-win. Don't be the next story on *Catfish: The TV Show.*

All of this said, I am not recommending that you assume the worst about all of your potential dates. In fact, I'm recommending the opposite. Give someone the benefit of the doubt unless you uncover one or more of the red flags listed. And, of course, be safe.

Chapter 20

ONLINE DATING SAFETY

Please keep these important safety tips in mind when online dating:

- Always meet in a public place. I recommend a bar/ lounge, a café or coffee shop, or the bar area of a restaurant.
- Do not allow someone to pick you up, thereby telling your date where you live.
- Do not accept a ride home if you're not feeling comfortable.
- Only exchange last names and other personal information like your email address if you choose to.
- Tell a friend where you're going and with whom.
- Make sure your cell phone is charged.
- Don't drink too much. You don't want to have impaired judgment with someone you don't know.
- Keep personal items in view at all times.

Most importantly, use your common sense. And don't forget to have fun!

WRAPPING UP WHAT WE'VE DISCUSSED SO FAR

So far, this book has been all about how to online date successfully. We discussed which photos to choose for your profile to make you stand out from the crowd. We then talked about how to write a concise and compelling "About Me" section that lets your best attributes shine without being too "braggy braggy," as I like to say. We talked about the art of differentiating yourself and how to put your best foot forward, keeping things light and positive and ending on a high note. We noted that it's important to state your deal-breakers in your profile but not to the point of saying everything you *don't* want in a partner. Rather, say what you do want. We went on to talk about the appropriate length of the profile, because there is a fine line between writing enough for people to get a sense of who you are but not writing so much that they pass you over out of sheer exhaustion from reading too much. We then put out the reminders that it's important to proofread, lest you make one error that turns many people off, and to be yourself, because even if that turns some people off, it will turn the right people on.

After we wrapped up the sections on the pictures and the profile, we talked about the actual searching and emailing process. We went over why, when searching, it's in no one's best interest for you to be too picky. In addition, it's important to change your search once in a while to perhaps catch some new people you hadn't seen before. We discussed the proper length and content of an email to ensure your best chances of getting a response, but we also talked about how oftentimes you will not get a response, and that's A-okay. It just wasn't meant to be.

We wrapped up the last section with some safety pointers and suggestions for types of places to meet for a first date. In the next section, I'll go into detail about that first date itself, because it's that date that will lead to another . . . and another . . . and another.

GATHER AROUND . . . IT'S STORY TIME!

The Pimple

I'm not sure how many of you used to watch *The Wonder Years*, but it was one of my favorite shows growing up. (And yes—I totally had a crush on Kevin Arnold . . . and perhaps still do.) In my opinion, one of the best episodes was the one where Kevin was really excited to see this old family friend, who, from her recent school photo, looked like she had blossomed into a total teenage hottie. But hark—Kevin woke up that fateful morning of the visit with the pimple of all pimples on his face. After applying pimple cream, a cold compress, and plenty of TLC, the pimple remained, bigger and badder than ever.

How did the day turn out? In TV-esque perfection, when the girl came to visit, she, too, had a massive pimple on her face. And the rest (of that episode anyway) was history.

Now, let's talk about me! About eight years ago, I was

on JDate (as you know, I was an early adopter), and I was really looking forward to meeting this guy Dave for a cocktail one Sunday evening. On the day of the date, I, of course, woke up with the worst cold ever. I had the sniffles, the red nose, the snot involuntarily running down my face—the works. Plus, my voice, as if it weren't nasal enough already, was even worse! So the question was this: To cancel or not to cancel? As many of us know, in the online dating world, people often get what I like to call "grass is greener syndrome," always looking for the next best thing out there. I didn't want my chance to meet Dave to pass me by if I cancelled. Who knew if or when we'd reschedule? So, I went on the date, tissues in hand and DayQuilled up. Until the moment he walked in (I was in rare form . . . I was early), I blew my nose like it was my job, making sure it would be as dry as a desert by the time he arrived.

And then Dave showed up. Nicely dressed. Very cute. The first words out of his mouth, you ask? "I'm sorry—I probably should have cancelled. I have a really bad cold." We laughed. We drank. We blew our noses. And then, lo and behold, we kissed. It's not like the other would catch our cold, after all.

And that was my Kevin Arnold picture-perfect pimple moment.

Section 7

THE FIRST DATE

In this section, you'll learn:

- Where to go on a first online date
- Whether to research your date before you meet or not
- What to wear on the first date
- Which questions to ask when meeting someone for the first time
- How to pay the bill
- How to gracefully end a particularly bad date

Chapter 21

WHERE TO GO

There is a section on several online dating sites that says, "My Perfect First Date." As I peruse people's responses, I'm overwhelmed by the number of people who say, "Dinner," or worse, "A long, romantic dinner." I don't know about you, but I'd be hard-pressed to devote two hours (or more) of my life to someone I've never met in person. Now, I'm not saying you can't have dinner with someone on the first date—quite the opposite. But instead of scheduling it ahead of time, you should just leave the option open. **You can always add dinner, but you can't take it back.**

On my first date with a previous long-term boyfriend, we made plans to meet after work for a drink. I had arranged to meet some friends at a party later that evening so that when the drink date was over (or if it wasn't going well), I had an excuse to leave. And I had actually been looking forward to the party! I warned my close friend, though, that if I ended up really liking this guy, I wouldn't be joining her and the others. Miracle of miracles, I did have fun, and I did like this guy. He asked me if I wanted to have dinner, and I agreed. (Although, I had actually already eaten after work since I didn't know when I'd have a chance to have dinner that night!) It ended up being a six-hour date.

It's okay to make other plans that aren't set in stone for after a date. You shouldn't schedule one-on-one plans, because you certainly don't want to stand up a friend if the date is going well, but it's great to have plans with a group or a party . . . or with a glass of wine on your couch watching *Beaches* if you're so inclined. That way, if the date doesn't go well, it's no biggie—you have other plans to look forward to and can still salvage the night. And if it does go well, you can continue the fun date. Is back-to-back booking okay? You bet it is.

So, rather than committing to dinner on your "Perfect First Date," how about this instead: "We start out with a drink, and perhaps a few hours, some dinner, and some flirtatious banter later, we're still enjoying each other's company." That sounds pretty perfect to me.

Also, for chivalry's sake (please don't let it die!), the gentleman should choose a location that is more convenient to the woman. She will appreciate a simple question such as, "Is there a particular area of town that works best for you?" If you're not familiar with the area she says, rather than asking her to choose a location (that puts a lot of pressure on the woman, especially if she doesn't know what sort of place you have in mind), you can instead give her a few options with the caveat, "But if you have something else you'd prefer, that would work as well." This way, she knows you put some thought into it. If you simply choose a location closer to you without asking, it appears to be a bit selfish because you're essentially saying, "I'm going to make the date convenient for me . . . and only me."

Q&A with Erika

Q: On Sunday, the Baltimore librarian date started with a handshake (initiated by her) and, three hours later, ended with her kind of darting across the street and me (in a poor application of your advice) calling after her somewhat pleadingly, "But should we meet up again?" To which she replied, "Sure—call me. No, email me." So clearly I don't think that's going anywhere. On Tuesday, the date with the nurse I mentioned went well, and I just asked her out again. But it may just wind up as a friend thing, too. We talked for like two and a half hours, and it started out well, then there was a lull in the middle, then it ended well. So how long should first dates be—should I be holding them to just like one hour, as opposed to interrogating these gals with my interviewing skills? But then again, if there isn't an initial spark, I'm sometimes hopeful that a spark may emerge.
—Geoffrey, 36, Arlington, VA

A: To answer your question about first date length, both of the dates you mentioned were much longer than I would suggest for a standard first date with someone you met online. It's always best to meet for coffee or a drink, have the "out" after an hour or so if you want it, but continue the date if you're not ready to leave yet. There's nothing wrong with leaving something to talk about on the second date. Also, I don't pick up on sarcasm very well, so I'm not sure if you were joking about interviewing these women, but definitely don't. Asking questions is great, but so is engaging in flirty banter and telling some stories. The interview-type stuff comes out naturally as you get to know someone better. The first date is really just to see if you have chemistry and to decide if you want to go on a second, "real" date. There are totally different rules for online dating versus dating someone you met in person already because clearly there's already chemistry in the latter situation since you agreed to go out. And I think you plan great dates . . . just wait for someone to earn and appreciate them.

Q: He asked me to dinner Sunday night—Chinese—which is really great, but I hate doing dinner on a first date. I like to do a more coffee/drinks thing so that there's the option of finishing up and ending it if it's not going well, or extending into grabbing a bite if it is. So how can I respond and finagle it into more of a drinks and less of a dinner thing? He ended his email with: "Would you be up for some Chinese food on Sunday evening?"
—Suzanna, 33, Philadelphia, PA

A: I actually just had this come up with another female client yesterday. First of all, don't panic! Here's what I told her, and I'll tell you the same. Just say something like this: "Meeting up Sunday night sounds great! I'm glad we're finally going to get to meet. Can we just plan on meeting for a drink (I may be having a late lunch that day), and then if we get hungry, we can grab a bite? No need to show you up with my mad chopsticks skills yet anyway. :) Maybe 7:30? Looking forward to it." It's only a partial lie, but it makes it a bit less committal. Remember—he is just trying to be a gentleman, so although I never recommend dinner on a first online date and would definitely only commit to a drink, it's not points against him.

Chapter 22

TO GOOGLE OR
NOT TO GOOGLE?

In this day and age, almost everyone has an online footprint . . . even Grandma. And whether through Google, LinkedIn, or Facebook, it's easy enough to track someone's entire life in 30 minutes or less (sounds oddly like a pizza delivery). When it comes to dating, the temptation to search before a first date is strong. "To Google or not to Google?" That is the question. And for most of us, the relevant question is now this: "To Facebook or not to Facebook?"

When it comes down to it, it's hard to resist the urge to Google or Facebook (I'm using it as a verb, in case you were wondering) your date once you have his or her full name staring you in the face. As I mentioned earlier, though, there is no need to exchange full names before the first date. It's as if the name is yelling, "Search me! Search me!" I'm not going to tell you that you can't look (who wouldn't?), but no matter what you find, try your hardest not to create a firm impression of this person in your mind before you meet. Unless you find out that he or she is a criminal (which actually happened to one of my clients who discovered that her date was wanted for securities fraud!), just go on the date, have fun, and try to put it all in the back of your mind.

When I was on JDate, I honestly didn't even think about Googling someone. Facebook was the first, and only, thing on my mind. Why would I Google someone to see the awards he got in college or his marathon time when I could Facebook him instead and see all of his pictures, credentials, and status updates? Google is, like, so 2005, right? Honestly, these days, who doesn't do a little online stalking—ahem—research?

No matter whether you do your pre-date "research" or not, please remember that this does not equal "friending." Friending someone on Facebook before the date is the kiss of death. Unless you already know each other, *do not* friend your date on Facebook either before you meet or immediately after the first date, even if it went really well. The last thing you want is to see all of your date's pictures with other people, whether exes or not, and get jealous before you're even together. Plus, there's something to be said for leaving some mystery. And if the date (or next date) doesn't go well, do you really want him or her knowing all of your business? I think not.

Lastly, if you decide to look up your date, feel free not to mention that you did, unless you're sure he or she won't put you in the "creep" category because of it. And if you're under about 30 years old, it's probably assumed that you looked. A little healthy online stalking = okay. Talking about the stalking = creepy. Know the difference.

Chapter 23

WHAT TO WEAR

Ah, the age-old question of what to wear on the first date . . .

Now, I'm not saying we should all be fashion mavens, but for the first date, it's important to put yourself together nicely. And doing this certainly doesn't have to be expensive. Heck—I still shop at Wet Seal, which is a store that's technically for teenagers!

Some first dates are right after work (say, happy hour), so that's easy—just go in your work clothes, albeit perhaps a spruced up version of your work clothes. But some dates aren't after work. I always have to laugh because on that six-hour first date I told you about, I wore a very heavy sweater dress because the party afterwards (the one I ditched) was an après-ski party. That was not a good first date outfit because it didn't show off my figure, and it had a huge cowl neck, making it seem like I didn't want to show any skin whatsoever. (I recently donated the dress. Good luck to the next wearer of it!)

For women, if you're coming from work, a nice business casual outfit works well. Try not to look too "business" and no fun, but a nice pair of pants or skirt and a top that shows off your shape but isn't too revealing works well. Also, try to wear colors like red or purple that show off your femininity a bit. Save the low-cut, curve-hugging outfits for going dancing Saturday night. When it's cold out, try not to wear anything like a huge turtleneck (or the dress I wore) because it makes you look very closed off from the guy's point of view, like he'd need a lock and key just to get to your neck. And in the winter, a good pair of tall boots can be very sexy.

For men, all I can say is that the iron is your friend. I can't think of anything worse than someone showing up for a date in clothes that are completely wrinkled. Heck—I'm not even saying you need to iron anything yourself. I often bring my shirts to get dry-cleaned because I really just want them pressed. Other than that, just go with your own style. Check your teeth, make sure there are no stains on your shirt, and you're good to go.

One final note: If you go on a date with someone you consider to be a bad dresser, remember that while his or her personality may not change, the clothes can, so try not to let it be a deal-breaker.

Now, go get dressed and enjoy your date!

Chapter 24

QUESTIONS, QUESTIONS, QUESTIONS

It's no secret that first dates are hard. There's no denying that. Whether it's the endless supply of sweat that you didn't know your body could produce, the awkward silences when you actually contemplate talking about how unseasonably cold it is outside, or the question of who pays the bill (we'll find out in the next chapter) that throws you off, we all know that first dates are often fairly anxiety inducing. One thing that makes them even harder is not knowing the right questions to ask.

Now, we all hope that the conversation flows naturally on a first date, pinging and ponging like Zhang Jike, an Olympic table tennis player in the London Olympics. (Yes—I'm a total ping-pong nerd.) But inevitably, most of us, even those who think we could have a conversation with a piece of broccoli if we had to, will be stumped at some point or another. Rather than running off to the restroom to plot your next conversation topic, it's a good idea to have a few questions in your back pocket just in case the sound of the gulping of your drink doesn't quite overpower the dreaded silence.

There are no objectively right or wrong questions to ask on a date, but the ones that have the most luck require more than a simple one-word answer. You want to get the person thinking, showing that you actually care. For example, rather than asking, "What do you do?" (perhaps the most boring question in the book), you could instead ask, "What made you decide to get into exotic bird-watching for a living?" or "How do you enjoy your job as a pediatrician? I imagine it must be very rewarding." The first question allows your date to simply say, "I'm a bird-watcher/doctor," but the other two require a bit more thought and introspection, leading to a more thoughtful conversation . . . and perhaps a second date.

Other questions that might come in handy:

- How was your day? (While often overlooked, this is a great conversation starter, with dates, friends, or colleagues.)
- What do you generally like to do after work?
- What made you decide to move to the area, and how do you like it?
- What kinds of things do you like to read? Have you read anything good lately that you would recommend?
- What is your perfect way to spend a Saturday or Sunday?

Remember that this is a date, not an interview, despite what poor Geoffrey in Arlington thought, so try to avoid acting like you're judging the other person based on his or her answers. (Maybe you are, but keep that to yourself!) It's best to stay away from the stereotypical interview questions, such as, "What is the hardest thing you've ever accomplished?" or "Was there ever a time when you were challenged to do something you felt was wrong?" These questions are scary, whether at an interview or on a date. Don't put the person on the spot. Rather, ask something that he or she already knows or can at least have a fun time thinking about. Also avoid very controversial topics, like politics, unless you're ready to open the floodgates.

Dating is about both talking and listening. The date should be a give and take, with you asking some questions and your date asking some questions. What you say is just as important as your ability to listen. And what will you be listening to? The answers to these fabulous questions you'll ask!

Q&A with Erika

Q: So I've been texting back and forth with this girl for a while now (kept having conflicting schedules), and we're finally getting to meet this Thursday. Can you give me some first date advice for meeting someone online? In the past first dates I've had, we talked about our experiences with OkCupid and Match. (Like, how many people we've met, bad/good experiences, etc.) Do you think that's something that shouldn't be brought up? Is there a certain length I should keep the date to, or does it just depend on how well the date is going? Any first date advice is much appreciated!
—David, 28, New York, NY

A: That is very exciting! If you're meeting someone for the first time from an online dating site, it should always just be for drinks or coffee, never dinner. As for the length, it's usually about an hour. If you're having a good time, though, obviously you'll want to stay longer and perhaps order some food.

In terms of what to talk about, I wouldn't lead with the question of how online dating is going, unless it's under the guise of how well this date is going compared to others, accompanied by a funny story. Otherwise, I would avoid this topic since your date may make assumptions based on the number of dates you've been on or how you speak about your other dates. Plus, no one likes to be compared. Just be yourself and be natural, and the conversation should flow. It's most important to talk about your hobbies and things you like to do to see if you have any of the same interests. And women like when you ask them questions—what she likes to do, etc. You'll know when you talk if you're clicking or not just based on how the conversation is going.

The first date is kind of like a screener to see if you want to take her out again, so keep the conversation light and fun (and a little flirtatious if you like). If, at the end, you do like her, it's best to tell her that you'd like to see her again so there's no question. Then, you can either line up the next date just then or follow up afterwards. (No three-day rule!) If you're not interested in seeing her again, then a simple "Nice meeting you" will do the trick. And please pay, no matter how it goes. It's the gentlemanly thing to do.

Chapter 25

CHECK, PLEASE!

You know the scenario well: The check comes. No one moves. You look at each other. You smile. The check sits there. This, my friends, is what we call a little game of "pick-up check."

The question is this: **Should a woman offer to split the bill on the first date?**

Notice that the question isn't **Should a man pay on a first date?** The answer to this question should be an unequivocal "yes." While I'm a huge advocate for women emailing men on the online dating sites, and I'll even dare to say that a woman should suggest meeting in person if the guy is trying to have an e-lationship, which we discussed earlier, I am a stickler for the old-fashioned tenet that the man should pay on the first date. That said, should the woman at least offer to pay?

When the bill comes, the woman has a few choices:

1. The reach (going for her wallet to see what happens)
2. The offer (saying "May I contribute?" or something similar)
3. The assumption (just saying "Thank you so much!")

Given that the date should only consist of a drink or

coffee, as we've discussed ad nauseam, and should not be too expensive, options #2 or #3 are the most appropriate. With #3, it avoids some of the awkwardness and you get to show your gratitude immediately, though it may seem a bit presumptuous to assume he's paying, which may not go over well. With #2, it's a polite gesture that he'll most certainly appreciate. I've always been a fan of the "May I contribute?" line that I listed above. Let's just hope he doesn't take you up on it!

Men, generally when women offer to pay on the first date, we don't want you to take us up on it. Even if we know there won't be a second date and feel slightly guilty for taking the free drink, deep down we still hope that you'll pay, because it's still a date, after all. The last thing you want is to accept our payment offer and then be labeled as "cheap." Yes—she offered, but when it comes to paying on a first date, yes almost always means no.

Now, of course, in some cases, for one reason or another, the woman will *insist* on paying and not back down until you let her. Sometimes if a woman is not interested in her date, she'll pay so she doesn't feel like she owes him anything. Ladies, you owe him nothing! It's just a date.

That said, I had one particularly memorable experience with the pick-up check game, and I'll tell you off the bat that the results weren't good. The scene: a JDate at a coffee shop called Tryst. Jason (I changed his name) and I planned to meet at 3:00 on a Sunday afternoon. When I got there, I saw someone who looked vaguely like the guy I was expecting, but he was deep in thought on his laptop, and he was drinking a nearly-finished coffee. Was this my date? I went over to him and asked, "Are you Jason?" It was, in fact, Jason. He had gotten there early to do some work. I certainly didn't mind that at all, but when the check came for my latte (a whopping $3 and change), he never even looked at it. Apparently he had already paid for his drink, so he took no responsibility for mine. Awkward, to say the least. Pick-up check fail.

Ideally, the man will reach for the check before the woman even has the chance to decide between the three options. Then, even if it's not a love connection, she'll tell her friends how generous he was. Let's avoid the game of pick-up check and end the date on a more positive note . . . planning the second date.

I also occasionally get questions from clients and friends about whether to use a "deal" on a date. Between Groupon and all of the other sites that offer coupons, at least half of my emails when I get up every morning are from the various daily deal companies vying to get some of my money for one of the deals that I'll accidentally let expire anyway. (Note to self: Unsubscribe.)

In 2011, I read an article in the *San Jose Mercury News* called "Attitudes about dating changing in this dour economy." The article says that it is now (well, back in 2011) socially acceptable to use these daily deals on a date:

> Match.com's Whitney Casey says new couples are also more willing to accept a date paying with a coupon from a daily deal site than they were in years past. In fact, five

years ago Casey did a study of Match.com daters, many who said they would rather a date's credit card be rejected than them offer to pay with a coupon. Today, coupon promotions are accepted ways of finding new places to eat or play on the cheap. "It's become really hip and cool," she says. "I think today nobody wants to get taken and paying full price for something is for fools."[5]

I beg to differ. I would say there is a definite right and wrong way to use a daily deal on a date.

Wrong way:

Woman: Oh, Benny! What a fabulous dinner! Thanks again for a lovely date.

Man: You bet. Ah, here comes the check. I don't want to forget to use my Groupon when I pay. $20 off—that's gold!

Woman (to self): Sigh. I thought I finally met someone who wasn't cheap.

Right way:

Man: Hey, Samantha! Want to go to Cava tomorrow for dinner? I bought a Groupon months ago and have been wanting to use it.

Woman: What a great idea! I love that place, and we can have an extra appetizer with the money we'll save!

Man (to self): Oh yeah—I'm awesome.

See the difference? Here's the rule of thumb:

- No Groupons on first dates.

- No spur-of-the-moment Groupon usage if you're trying to impress someone.
- If you've planned the outing in advance *because* of the Groupon, then it's another story, and you're good to go.

Now, I'm not saying you should stop buying the daily deals. Many of them are amazing and worth it. But before you try to use it on a date, think to yourself, "How will this come off—as hip and in-the-know or as cheap?" If there's any chance it might come off as the latter, save it for another day. You must like the place if you bought the deal, so now you get to go back!

Q&A with Erika

Q: I bought the movie tickets because I got to the theater first. He treated me to popcorn and then dinner, and I got the ice cream. What do you think about the girl treating? I personally like to be treated. I was used to being spoiled like that with an ex. But then again, I paid him back in tears and heartache! Anyway, just curious as to what you think.
—Shauna, 38, Baltimore, MD

A: For your etiquette question, the way it worked out yesterday was okay. He could have just as easily gotten to the theater first and bought the tickets, and he probably appreciated that you did. Then, with him getting popcorn and dinner, it was a very nice gesture that you got the ice cream. My personal thoughts are that the guy should treat for the first few dates (but, like I said, I think he pretty much treated yesterday), and then you can offer to get some things. Men, of course, also like to occasionally be treated, so if you decide going in that you'll buy something, I'd say in a cute way, "And ice cream's on me." But there's no right or wrong. Since he paid most yesterday, I wouldn't worry about it. He seems like a gentleman. It's always awkward at the beginning, so it's not just you. As a final note, I always hate the gesture of splitting credit cards at dinner. One person buying one thing and the other buying something else is the preference. Splitting cards just screams "friend zone."

Chapter 26

CHECK, PLEASE! (BUT THIS TIME IN A DIFFERENT WAY)

You're on a date. It's going just okay. Actually, no it's not. You're bored. He lied in his profile. Her jokes are offensive. You got into an argument over some spilled wine. He was rude to the waiter. She thought it was polite to spit out her gum and keep it behind her ear for later. He started talking about a potential Martian invasion and possible future wars between humans and aliens. Whatever the reason, you want out.

And herein lies the question: Is there a polite, socially acceptable way to end a bad date and extricate yourself quickly and gracefully?

Now, I'm not necessarily talking about Barney Stinson's Lemon Law. (If you didn't watch *How I Met Your Mother*, now might be a good time to look it up.) I'm just talking about a courteous gesture that indicates that the date is over.

I once went on a JDate to play ping-pong. (I know I've mentioned my obsession with ping-pong before. It's not like I own five of my own paddles or anything . . . just three.) When I got there, I couldn't find him. Why, you might ask? Well, he was about 50 pounds heavier than his JDate picture and stated weight had indicated. I could talk for hours about the reasons not to lie online. It wasn't what he looked like at all that bothered me. I was annoyed that my date had lied, but I was already there, so I figured I'd give him the benefit of the doubt. It soon became clear, though, that he was also exceedingly boring (like, pulling teeth boring) and a poor sport when he lost to me in ping-pong. Three strikes for him, and I was outta there. I told him that my workout earlier in the day had really taken it out of me and that I had to go home.

Did I do the right thing? Maybe. In hindsight, while extremely difficult to do, it might have been more appropriate to say that I was disappointed that he had misrepresented his appearance. But what's done is done.

When it comes to a bad date, first determine the nature of "bad." Is it "creepy" bad or just "no sparks" bad? If it's the latter, then your best bet is to stick it out, at least for one glass of whatever you're drinking. An alcoholic beverage can't necessarily hurt, either. It may actually loosen you both up. Who knows? You might even start to like each other! Plus, the worst that could happen is that you get a funny story out of it. "Remember that time when I went out with a guy from JDate who had taken me out six years prior, but I didn't recognize him? I didn't like him then, and I certainly didn't like him now!" I'm so glad I stuck that one out since I'm still telling the story to this day, and it even made it into my book!

For the "creepy" bad date (other variants are "scary" bad,

"offensive" bad, "mean" bad—you get the idea), the best bet is to (gulp!) be honest. This is definitely the most awkward choice, but it's also the most mature. "You know, I just don't think we're clicking. It was very nice to meet you, but I don't want either of us to waste our time, so I thought I'd say that to give us the option to go do something else tonight."

Telling a white lie (you're not feeling well, you ate some bad cheese, you forgot about a work function you have to attend, you're really tired, etc.) to get out of a date, like I did, isn't usually the smartest move. You may cross paths with this person again, which could make this choice pretty awkward. Your date may not have gotten the hint and may try to ask you out again, and the lie will become apparent by your present lack of interest. No, a little white lie never killed anyone, but if you're comfortable enough to use the line "I just don't think we're clicking," it's a better, more honest approach.

So, while there's no dating Lemon Law, if your date starts discussing the pros of dogfighting, encouraging you to add goldfish to your diet, or coughing in your face without any regard for your personal space, it's more than okay to admit you're not a match and move on.

Chapter 27

PRACTICE MAKES . . . BETTER

When I was younger, I took piano lessons. Did I practice? Nope. Can I play the piano today? Not really. I still have to think about "Every Good Boy Does Fine" and "Good Boys Do Fine Always" or "Great Big Dogs Fight Animals," as my teacher taught me. (For those who have no idea what I'm talking about, those are mnemonics to remember the notes on the treble and bass clef, respectively.)

Later in life, when I decided that I wanted to sing, which is something I still really love to do, I wished I had actually listened to my teacher and parents (don't tell them I said that). While I certainly never had any desire to be a concert pianist or anything (my fingernails are way too long for that anyway), practicing would have helped me later when I discovered which form of music I wanted to pursue.

You're probably thinking, "I thought I was reading a book about online dating. What does practicing the piano have to do with dating?" In life, practicing makes you better for when that thing comes along that you really want to pursue. And in this case, that thing is a future date.

A friend once wrote to me:

So . . . I just took down my online dating profile because I started dating someone a few weeks ago and we DTRed* last night. I didn't meet him online, but I do think that I was a lot more comfortable going on dates with him because I'd been getting a lot of practice with the online dates, figuring out how to be slightly less awkward at ending dates and really identifying what was important to me and which behaviors to look for that signaled that the person had the characteristics that I was looking for. Everyone knows the old adage that "practice makes perfect," but I don't know if a lot of people really think about how much that can be applied to date-like interactions, which can be really complex. I really do think it helped build up my confidence and comfort level with guys.

*DTR = "Define the relationship. When two people discuss their mutual understanding of a romantic relationship (casual dating, serious boyfriend, etc)." Thanks, Urban Dictionary![6]

I couldn't agree more. Now, I'm not saying to go out with just anyone to get some practice, but it's important to remember that going on dates can only help define what you're looking for, and perhaps more importantly, what you're not looking for, in a partner. It can also, as my friend pointed out, help you hone your conversational skills. While every date may not lead to a trip down the aisle, each will fill your toolbox with useful skills to apply the next time.

I see many people peek into speed-dating events or quickly scan a page of Match.com search results for 30 seconds and decide on the spot that no one there interests them. If you've already committed the time (and often money), it's worth joining and meeting new people, even if only to become friends, while practicing the art of flirting, engaging in witty banter, and making conversation with a broad range of people. And when you finally meet the man or woman you've had your eye on for a while, you'll know that you're fully equipped to make a great impression.

So take it one date at a time. Practice will never make it perfect. We're still talking about dating here, so there's always going to be an element of awkwardness. But practice will make it better, for sure.

Chapter 28

WHAT TO DO AND WHAT NOT TO DO

Let's actually start with what not to do. (I always like to end on a positive note . . . and a major, not minor, note when I sing.)

For National Etiquette Week back in May of 2012 (who knew there was such a thing?), the dating site HowAboutWe .com[7] reported on the "Top 10 Worst First Date No-Nos," and what they found was spot-on.

1. **Having your phone out or texting**

   It doesn't get worse than this. Nothing screams "I'm waiting for something better to come along" more than a cell phone on the table at the ready. A corollary to this one is actually answering your phone or responding to a text on the date. Try (as hard as it may be) to put your phone in your bag or your pocket for the entirety of the date. Obviously if there are unforeseen circumstances, like you're expecting a call from a child or a doctor, it's more than okay to tell your date that you may need to take a call.

2. **First date sex**

   Generally, for men, it makes you look like you only want one thing (and maybe you do). For women, it makes you look like you're somewhat easy. It is definitely a double standard, unfortunately.

3. **Talking about your ex**

   If you say nice things about your ex, it looks like you're still not over him or her. And if you say mean things, it looks like you're still not over him or her *and* you're bitter. Lose-lose. Plus, people don't want to feel like they are being compared to someone else on the first date (or ever, for that matter).

4. **Being late (more than 15 minutes)**

   People run late—it happens. But if it does, and by more than about 15 minutes, please call to let your date know before the start of the date. Texting is insufficient. If you're just running a few minutes late, texting is okay, but there is still a need to notify the other person. No being late without a warning.

5. **Being rude to a server**

   No snapping your fingers, no yelling for the waiter or waitress, and no treating the servers like second-class citizens. Red flag!

6. **Drinking too much**

   People have a tendency to divulge secrets or commit dating no-no #2 (or likely both) when too much alcohol is involved. Don't let it be you.

7. **Splitting the bill or letting the woman pay**

   You remember the game of pick-up check. The guy should pay on a first date. Whether you like each other or not, it's still a date, after all, and chivalry is not dead.

8. **Work talk**

   It is certainly okay to discuss work, but not for the entire date, especially if you don't like your job. Talking about work the whole time may put you in the "friend zone" unnecessarily because you seem more like a colleague or an interviewer than a potential love interest.

9. **Mother talk**

   Leave your mom out of the date. Especially for men—it may make you look like a bit of a mama's boy. (Sorry!) Being close to your family, of course, is wonderful, and that should definitely be shared.

10. **Talking about marriage**

   Great—you like each other! The last thing you want to do is to bring up marriage and scare the other person away. The same goes for talking about, or naming, your future children. You may laugh, but it happens.

A few others from the report were:

- Bad breath
- Not tipping well
- Talking about yourself too much
- Being "fake" or not being yourself
- Smoking

Now that we've gotten the no-nos out of the way, let's discuss some helpful tips for a great first date. Just as important as knowing what *not* to do is knowing what *to* do on a first date to increase your chances of making it to the all-important second date.

1. **Ask questions.**

   I used to go on so many dates where the guy talked the entire time. Even if I tried to get a word in edgewise, the conversation somehow had a way of settling on him again. I know the art of asking questions, but sadly, some people don't. I remember one date in particular with a guy we'll call Paul. It wasn't until the check came for our drinks that he said, "Oh, so tell me about you." At that point, I was already turned off. Conversations need to consist of some give and take, especially on a first date, so remember to ask some thoughtful questions.

2. **Be optimistic and happy.**

   It's important to have a good attitude on a date, even if your happy face is only covering up the fact that this is your third date this week, and the rest have been, well, sub-par. People can smell negativity, and it creates an unpleasant aura on a date. In other words, try not to be jaded, and if you are, fake it 'til you make it. (Or, take a break from dating until you're really ready to get back out there.) A simple smile goes a long way.

3. **Discuss issues that are important to you.**

   I'm not talking about politics or anything, but if there's something that you're passionate about, it's going to come out sooner rather than later, so it might as well be sooner. A lot of my female clients worry that a guy will judge her for her interests. One in particular takes a pottery-making class. She was concerned that a guy might find that lame and grandma-like (her words, not mine). Who cares? It's what you like to do, so own it. If a guy couldn't handle that I like doing my daily crossword puzzle, religiously watching *Glee*, and reading the occasional *US Weekly* (okay, okay—I read it every week), then he wouldn't be getting the whole package.

4. **Offer to walk her to where she's going.**

Generally, it'll be dark out by the time you end your date, especially in the months during fall and winter. Men, it's important to offer to walk your date to where she's going—her car, the entrance to the train station, or wherever it may be. If she declines the offer, you still did your part by asking.

Much of a first date is less about the actual words you say and more about your attitude. Are you listening, being nice, and making the effort? These things go a long way. Even if you're perfect for each other on paper, the attitude makes all the difference.

GATHER AROUND . . . IT'S STORY TIME!

Four's a Crowd

I live for awkward moments. I don't get embarrassed easily . . . or ever. I like to point out the obvious. This all adds up to a fun and interesting dating life.

A fun thing to know about me is that I love to be on stage. Put an audience and a microphone in front of me, and I'm a happy lady. In addition to being a love guru,

I also occasionally perform in a group where we get on stage and tell true stories that have happened to us in life. The stories are usually pretty humorous, and some are downright ridiculous.

Well, I was very proud to have been chosen to perform in one of these shows, and because of this, I decided to invite everyone I had recently been on dates with—Rob, Jonathan, and Max. (For their protection, mainly from embarrassment, I changed the names.) For some reason, 1) I didn't think they'd all come, and 2) I certainly didn't think they would all ask if I wanted to go out after the performance. Wrong and wrong.

Not knowing what to do, I figured honesty was the best policy, so I said, "Okay, so this is awkward, but I've been out with all three of you recently. Just putting that out there." No one seemed fazed by this. Okay . . .

So the four of us—Erika and her entourage—went to get drinks. One drink led to two, two drinks led to three, and the four of us had a fabulous time. All of the men got along swimmingly! I guess that's a testament to my taste, but I thought it was hilarious. Then this question arose: Who would take me home? While I allowed one to ride in a cab home with me, I very contently snuggled up with only one man that night—Scruffy.

Section 8

THE FOLLOW-UP

In this section, you'll learn:

- When to follow up with someone after a date
- What means to use for following up after a date
- What to do if you're not sure about your feelings for someone after the date

I used to play tennis, and the main thing the instructor always told me was to make sure to follow through. Even if I hit the ball just the right way, using my two-handed backhand (though I finally learned to do a one-handed backhand when playing squash), if I didn't follow through, the great shot would have been for naught. The same thing goes for dating.

Congratulations—you got the date! Whether it went well or it didn't, the final thing I want to talk about is the follow-up. What's the point of a great first date if there's not a second?

Chapter 29

THE THREE-DAY RULE?

She said yes! She's amazing! She's incredible! I would have never asked her out without you. Thank you! Thank you!
—Scott, 38, Ames, IA

You go on a first date Tuesday night, and you think it went pretty well. In fact, you're sure it went pretty well. I mean, why else would your prospective new lover constantly let his or her knee graze yours all night or share your drink as if you'd known each other for more than, oh, 45 minutes? You go home happy. Wednesday morning comes and goes, and by Wednesday afternoon at around 3:00, you think the potential new relationship is doomed. It's been 17.26 hours, and you haven't even gotten a measly text!

The advent of modern technology—texting, instant messaging, and email—has completely changed the "three-day rule" into more like a "three-hour rule." So many relationships end before they even begin because no one knows the answer to the simple question: How soon do you follow up after a date?

A survey performed by the company LoveGeist was commissioned by Match.com in mid-2011, and it found that after a first date on a Saturday evening, most daters will get in touch by 11:48 on Monday morning with a call or text. Thus, 1.52 days is now the average time spent waiting for a follow-up message.[8] The three-day rule is now cut in half! As a side note, I don't, however, recommend a first date on a Saturday night, especially a first online date. A weeknight or Sunday evening date works well, and then if you want to see each other again, you can plan for the coveted Friday or Saturday night slot when you already know you have some chemistry.

We are all basically surgically attached to our phones anyway. I know someone who texted from the hospital bed just minutes after she had a baby (Hi, Kim!), and we all know someone (and that person likely stares at us in the mirror) who checks his or her email every morning on the phone before even getting out of bed. When it comes down to it, if you like someone, it's so easy to get in touch. If you wait the antiquated three days, it's already a foregone conclusion that you're probably just not that into the other person.

In most cases, if he's interested, the man will contact the woman after the date to ask her out again. But I do encourage the woman to send a "thank you" text the day after the date. Why not remind your date of you the next day? Assuming he also had a great time, it'll put a smile on his face and give him the "nudge" he needs to know that you want to stay in contact with him.

The rules are simple: If you like someone and want to make plans for a second date, then make the contact in a timely fashion. A short and sweet text, email, or call will work. And ladies, if he has the courtesy to ask you out again and you're not interested, please do the kind thing and thank him, using the honest answer that you just didn't feel a spark. Ignoring it will only make a possible future encounter (remember—it's a small world) that much more awkward.

And there we have it—the three-day rule debunked. Somehow the "1.52-day rule" just doesn't quite have the same ring to it. Let's call it the "36-hour rule" and be on our way.

Q&A with Erika

Q: I had a nice afternoon date yesterday with someone from JDate. We had two beers together over about 90 minutes (I paid, of course). From my perspective, I thought the conversation went quite well. We know some people in common and both are active and enjoy bike rides. We talked about riding together some weekend. Oh, and get this: Both our parents were married on the exact same day—June 26, 1966. Perhaps it's a sign.

As we were getting ready to get up, I suggested maybe getting together for dinner one day this week. She seemed into the idea but cautioned that she has a trial coming up (yup, she's an attorney) and her schedule is touch and go.

I have one question on how to proceed—should I continue to email her through JDate, text her, or give her a call? My sense tells me that phoning is best, but I can sometimes be awkward on the phone so am nervous about preserving my impression on her. What do you think?

—Danny, 39, Houston, TX

A: That is pretty incredible that your parents were married on the same day! As for how to proceed, I agree that calling would be the best option, with an email being a good second choice. Do you have her personal email address? That would be preferable to a JDate email, but either would be okay. If you do email her on JDate, ask for her personal email address so you can email that way instead. And if you do call, I certainly understand your concern—most people are awkward on the phone! Just make sure to set the date and don't chit-chat too much. That way, even if it's awkward, you still have the date on the calendar, which is what you want.

Q: I met Jessie yesterday. We spent about an hour and a half together, even though we only met for drinks. We both agreed to go out again. My question to you is whether I should text or call her, and when? I was thinking that a phone call is more personal. My plan was to text her tonight telling her that I had a good time, and I would call her tomorrow to set up another date. Another scenario is that I just call her tomorrow and tell her I had a good time and make plans for another date, all in one phone call. I could also just call her tonight and accomplish the same thing instead of waiting a day. What do you think is best, or do you have a better suggestion?
—Jared, 37, Alexandria, VA

A: First of all, I'm glad the date went so well! I like your first plan the best—text her today (you don't need to wait until tonight) telling her you had a good time and that you'll call tomorrow to set up the next date. Then, when you do call, she'll see that you're a man of your word. It'll work well.

Q: Is there a specific time or day when I should post my profile? I also wanted to ask about first meetings for coffee or a drink—any certain days/times it is better to do this? Earlier on a Saturday, say, rather than later? I know you said there are no dumb questions. ;)
—Laurie, 46, Tampa Bay, FL

A: To answer your first (not dumb!) question, there is no best time of week to post your profile, but posting it at night will get it more immediate visibility. Also, a lot of people tend to go online on Sunday night. For the coffee/drink date, any night of the week but Friday or Saturday will work best. And that's to protect you in case you don't hit it off. Saturday or Sunday afternoon coffee is nice, too. I just happen to like the drink date since it's a little more relaxing . . . liquid courage!

A NOTE ON TEXT MESSAGING, OR TEXTIQUETTE, AFTER THE FIRST DATE:

As you already read, my favorite use of the text after the first date is the "thank you" text, for both men and women. If you had a good time and want to see this person again, send a text saying thanks. It can be flirty, funny, or just plain sweet. Especially for women, if a guy paid for the date (and, as you know, on the first date, he should), he'll appreciate another thank you, either over text or email. If your date also had a great time, it'll put a smile on his or her face to see your name pop up on the phone.

What not to do at this stage: have a long, detailed conversation over text. (It's just too much.) Also, please don't use pet names over text yet. You just met!

Q&A with Erika

Q: I wanted your opinion on a situation with a guy I'm dating. Well, we've been on three dates. Okay, here's the scenario: I met him on Match.com a few weeks ago. Our first date was just drinks—fun, good convo, etc. On the way out, he said he wanted to get together again and followed up. A week later, we had date number two. We met in Old Town, walked around, took the water taxi to National Harbor, had dinner, and took the water taxi back. He planned it, and it went well. We split that night without making plans again but agreed to chat soon. The following Tuesday (a few days later), I got two tickets to the Skins game through some partnership at work and asked him to come along. We had what I thought was a really fun night. Got a few kisses and hugs, and I went home thinking there will be a next date.

I got a text today thanking me for the tickets, saying it was fun and to have a nice week—no invite

or suggestion of a next date. The text had a smiley face and exclamation points and all that so it seemed positive, but that "have a nice week" comment is grating on my nerves. Is this an overreaction? Normal guy behavior? Or just a simple "he had fun but he's just not that into me?"
—Shelley, 36, Alexandria, VA

A: If only men came with an instruction manual, huh? I wouldn't read too much into the last text; however, you're not wrong to be annoyed. Any woman would be. But remember that 1) he did come to the game, 2) he did kiss you, and 3) he did reach out after the game, even if it was a lame text. Three positive things. And he wasn't required to do any of them. He did them because he wanted to. I would respond with something cute, like, "You bet. Thanks for being my arm candy Monday night. Now that we've been to a pro football game, where do we go from here? ;)" Obviously tweak it to what makes you feel comfortable. Then the (foot)ball is in his court.

Chapter 30

INDECISION

Just wanted to thank you again for being the "nudge" I needed to get onto Match and for helping me create a successful profile. Much to my surprise, I've been dating one of the first guys who responded for about eight weeks now and have never been so happy/had so much fun. And I didn't even know if I liked him at first! We're headed to NYC for a long weekend together next weekend. Anyway, so, so glad you and I connected and I can't thank you enough!!

—Emily Ann, 40, Bethesda, MD

What if you're not sure whether you want to go on a second date with someone? The date was fine. There weren't sparks flying or fireworks exploding, but it wasn't the worst date you've ever been on, either. Your date wasn't rude to the server or offensive in any way, and you did have things in common, but you're just not sure how you feel. I'd suggest giving it another shot.

I have certainly been on my fair share of bad dates. Back in 2005, I went on a first date to a Mexican restaurant for dinner. (I know I've mentioned this about 100 times already, but try to avoid dinner on the first date. Oops.) At any rate, my date was (how shall I put this?) B-O-R-I-N-G. I consider myself to be a pretty darn engaging person who can talk to just about anyone. But there were silences, and awkward ones at that. As I chomped away on my fajitas, I was planning in my head what I would say for the next half an hour at least. Finally, the date came to a close. I thought to myself that he was a nice enough guy, but that was about it.

The next day, in usual Erika-style, I sent my standard "thank you" email, which is, of course, what we did in the "olden days" before texting became the norm. He did pay for my meal, after all. I figured this email would be the end of our communication. But then, against all odds, he responded saying that he had a good time and then wrote something funny at the end of his email. I thought, "Hmm . . . this guy wasn't funny at all on our date. Interesting." And so, the emails continued, and they became wittier as the hours passed. And then they got downright cute . . . until he asked me out again. What was a girl to do? While I didn't have a great time on the date, this guy seemed interested, I knew he could at least communicate in written form, and, well, I was free the night he asked. Oh, and I love baseball. (He asked me to go to a Nationals game with some friends.) Why not?

The day of the second date rolled around, and I remember sitting at my apartment building's pool studying for the GMAT with a friend. I kept telling her that I was not looking forward to this date. The hours passed, I finally decided to get ready at the last second, and off I went. We met in the Metro, and he wasn't as bad as I had remembered. In fact, he was kind of cute. When we got to the game, his friends were really friendly and inclusive of me. And then, believe it or not, this guy was really funny! It was as if I was on a date with a different person. We had a great night and even went out after the game. I liked this guy.

I found out many months later that he was nervous—very nervous—on the first date. We ended up dating for a year and a half. While he wasn't the right guy for me in the long run, I was so glad that I had gone out on the second date—hence the **Rule of Two.** Many people get nervous, or as I used to affectionately call myself on dates where I was trying to impress someone, "Weird Erika."

The moral? Unless someone spits on you, picks his or her nose, offends you in some unforgivable way, or does something to make it undeniably clear that you are not meant to be, it can't hurt to go on the second date. You never know what comes after the first unless you try.

Another way to look at it is to think to yourself, "What's the whole point of dating anyway?" (Before you shut this book in shock and awe, just trust me on this one.) Not that I take Urban Dictionary as gospel (I'd have some problems if I did!), but when it comes to the definition of "dating," the usually off-color site does a surprisingly good job of defining the word. The first definition on the site says that dating is " . . . To be in the early stages of a relationship where [you] go out on dates to find out what each other is like, as a prelude to actually being a fully-fledged couple."[9] Notice that the definition isn't "going out once to determine if this person will be your soul mate." This is where many people get confused.

Clients and friends ask me all the time whether they should go on a second date since they're not sure whether they were really into the other person, either for personality or physical attraction reasons, after the first date. They reason that they don't want to lead the other person on, making him or her think that this might be the beginning of a relationship when, in fact, the next date would be "just to see" if there's any potential there.

While in theory this makes sense, I argue that the whole point of dating is to get to know people to see if you want to start a relationship with them. The definition above even states that people date "to find out what each other is like." It's often the case that we're not sure how we feel after a first date. Of course, it's sometimes clear that you have a major spark, or alternately, that you can't stand the other person. (The guy I once went out with who literally sulked—yes, literally—when I beat him at ping-pong certainly made the decision easy for me.) It's often too hard after just one date, which is likely only an hour or so long, to decide if this person will ultimately be the mother or father of your children! My point is this: It's okay to see someone again just to see whether he or she is a good fit. You're not leading someone on—you're just dating!

As in my story before, it's more than okay not to know after the first date how you feel about someone. Remember, you don't have to make life-altering decisions after one measly date, like what kind of wedding china you're going to get or whether to cut Aunt Mildred from the guest list. Simply ask yourself this question: Do I want to have another conversation with this person? If the answer might be yes (or even if you're not sure), you have nothing to lose by giving it another shot. It's just dating, after all.

Q&A with Erika

Q: I'm doing all right with dating—just at the moment, wondering the value of spending the time and money on a second date if I wasn't blown away on the first date. Thoughts?
—Preston, 44, New Orleans, LA

A: To answer your question about whether or not to take someone on a second date if you weren't enthralled on the first, I'd say that it depends. If you think there might be some connection but you have to get to know her better, it's worth the second date. If she is definitely not what you're looking for because of a few things—she was rude, you didn't find her attractive, you had clashing views on something important—obviously, it's not worth it. Remember, though, that people are not always themselves on the first date. In terms of the time and money aspect, while I think you come up with some of the best date ideas ever (really), I would cool it on the creative (and sometimes expensive/time-consuming) first dates and, rather, take her for a drink or coffee, and plan to spend just an hour or so unless you really like each other. Even for the second date, you don't have to go crazy—a casual dinner would be just fine. That way, you're not pulling out the big guns (and bucks) before you know if she appreciates it. The really creative date ideas you have should be used on someone who is definitely worth it.

Q: As I mentioned, my Wednesday date went well. At the end of the date, he said, "We should do it again sometime." Since I liked him, I replied, "Absolutely!" Well, last night, he responded to my thank you note and said that he enjoyed the conversation too, and again said, "We should do it again sometime." I would definitely be interested in a second date. What is the best way to respond to that email? I had thought of saying, "We should go to a Nats game" (since he is a big baseball fan), but there isn't one for a while. Any thoughts on how to approach the vague invite?
—Allison, 41, Washington, D.C.

A: Ah—the vague invite. It's so annoying, isn't it? The fact that he responded to your thank you note at all means that he probably likes you enough to go out again. He wouldn't have responded otherwise. The terrible thing most people do is just ignore it if they're not interested, which I was never a fan of. I'd respond, "Great! My schedule's filling up for the next week, so do you want to say Wednesday or Thursday if you're around?" (Obviously, fill that in with whatever dates work best for you.) That way, it's not too pushy, but you're showing him that you are the busy and popular woman that you are! If he does, in fact, want to see you again, he'll either choose one of the dates you listed or propose an alternative. If he still answers vaguely, then there's not much more you can do.

Q: I am such a novice—do you think there needs to be chemistry ASAP? Did you go out a couple of times with most folks who seemed to be pleasant and compatible, even if bells and whistles did not go off? I am friendly, so unless someone hates liberals and is a control freak (it has happened to me), I am often the one making the "decision" in the end. Any advice is good. —Melinda, 55, Cape May, NJ

A: To answer your questions, I do not necessarily think there needs to be chemistry ASAP. People are often nervous on a first date and end up being a diluted or censored version of themselves, so giving someone a second chance if you're on the fence (as long as you didn't hate him, of course) is generally a good idea. Try to think of it as less of a hard "decision" and more of a fluid "get to know each other" process.

Chapter 31

JUST NOT THAT INTO YOU?

If, after giving it thought, you decide that a second date isn't in the cards (which, of course, is more than okay), how do you let someone down in a kind manner?

The Scene: Islay Bar & Grill, a first date from OurTime.com (a site for singles aged 50+)

The Cast: Janet, 58, avid skier and hiker, and Robert, 61, steak-lover and fan of NASCAR and extreme fighting competitions

The Exit Interview:

Janet: "He was just okay. We didn't have a lot in common, and the attraction wasn't there for me, unfortunately. I'm glad we met, but I think it was pretty clear that this was our first and last date."

Robert: "Wow. Janet is the woman I have been waiting for. She listened to every word I said about professional auto racing, and she got two glasses of wine, so that must mean she wanted to stay longer. I think I'll email her tomorrow to ask her out again. I don't see any reason why she'd say no."

This scenario occurs a lot, and the disappointed party is

not limited to either gender—it happens to all of us. It's not the end of the world, though. Seeing if you have a mutual connection with someone is what dating is all about. Unfortunately, sometimes one of you just doesn't feel it. It's how you handle yourself afterwards that really matters.

If your date wants to see you again, you'll usually get an email or text. (Sadly, for many people, the phone's gone out the window these days. But a call is still a wonderful and classy choice . . . the choice many women prefer.) If you're not interested, you have four choices: 1) Agree to go out with him or her again, 2) politely decline with a white lie, 3) politely decline with the truth, or 4) ignore him or her. Assuming you really do not want to go out with the person again, the best option is the third choice above. No one can be upset with you for politely telling the truth. But it's all in how you say it. I probably should save this email since I give it to clients so often:

> It was really nice meeting you, and thanks again for the drink. Unfortunately, I just didn't think we clicked the way I'd want us to, but I think you're really great and hope to run into you again soon.

Or

> It was really nice meeting you, and thanks again for a lovely evening. Unfortunately, I didn't feel the connection I was looking for, but I wish you the best of luck!

Not bad, right? It's truthful (unless you don't think the person is great at all), gets the point across, and there won't be any miscommunication.

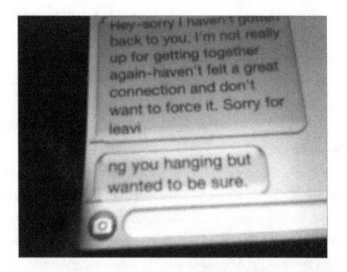

What if someone wants to convey this message but lacks the tact to do so properly? A friend of mine received the text message you just read, saying, "Hey—sorry I haven't gotten back to you. I'm not really up for getting together again—haven't felt a great connection and don't want to force it. Sorry for leaving you hanging but wanted to be sure." Remember that this was after just one date, and my friend texted him to say thanks and indicate that she would be interested in seeing him again, not because she was in love, but because she wanted to give it another shot. He sent this text about a week later, well beyond when he should have. It's pretty clear that he lacked sensitivity, and now not only does she know he's just not that into her, but she doesn't even like him as a person. As I said, no one should get angry with you for being honest, but please do try to do it nicely.

A friend of mine once one emailed me this dilemma of hers:

That reminds me, I went out with the French guy from online—the one I had a nice e-lationship with. The date was fine. I don't really have complaints, but I also do not have butterflies whatsoever, not even moths fluttering around. I think the attraction was not there. He has now been texting, but I couldn't get myself to text him back yesterday. I just don't think I want to hang out again. Is that bad? Should I give it another shot? Also, if not, do I need to let him know that nicely or do I just not write back? Ugh—I never know what to do!

My response:

Well, I'm glad the e-lationship with the guy ended and you finally met. Did he at least have a sexy accent? ;) Unfortunately, only you know whether there's enough potential to go out with him again. If you think there's even a small chance, it can't hurt to give it another shot. Some people do get nervous on the first date, and attraction definitely grows the more you get to know and like someone's personality. But that one is up to you. As for letting him know versus not, in this day and age, as you know, most people do not get back to someone after the first date if they don't want to go out again. Given that he did text, you could let it go, which I'm sure is what most people would do. But the better, much more mature, response would be to say, "I had a fun time the other night. Not sure I felt the spark I was looking for, but thanks again for a nice evening!" That way, it's honest, and if you ever run into each other, he can't fault you for being truthful. I've found that it's typically the best policy because the non-response gets awkward sometimes, and with this city being so small, you're bound to run into people. Let me know what you decide to do.

So be honest . . . and be nice.

Q&A with Erika

Q: I called her Thursday night and got her cell's VM— left her a confident and funny message and received no response at all. It's kind of disappointing that after spending five and a half hours with her over two dates, she isn't even responding now. What's the deal? —Neil, 42, Chicago, IL

A: If she hasn't called back, or at least responded in some way, all I have to say is that she is very rude. Lately, as much as I hate to say it, rude seems to have become the norm. I have this conversation a lot, not just with dating but with other things, like responding to emails and calling people back. People for some reason think they have no obligation to do that. And after two dates where you presumably treated her (yes?), she should at the very least acknowledge that you called, even if just with an email, or even a text, back. I'm really sorry that happened. It does, however, show you something about her character. On to bigger and better things.

CONCLUDING REMARKS

Throughout all of the trials and tribulations of online dating, it's important to remember one thing: Rome wasn't built in a day, and neither is the process of finding the love of your life. Many people go online or go to a speed-dating event and expect to find their "one and only" simply by signing up or logging in. Unfortunately, it's not that easy, and it will take some time. But don't worry—all of the effort isn't for naught. Let's look at a few steps in the process:

- **Signing up for an online dating site for the first time**
  Remember, finding the love of your life takes time and work.

- **Going on a first date**
  While you always hope that each one may be your last first date, just go in looking for great conversation and some things in common.

- **Going to a social event**
  It's okay if your future spouse doesn't sweep you off your feet at the event. Just go to have a good time and meet some new people.

- **Going to a wedding**
  I know they say weddings are a great place to meet

people, and one of my best friends actually moved across the country to be with a wonderful man she met at a wedding, but it's rare that the circumstance works out as well as it did for them. If you're going to a wedding solo, just enjoy the event, stuff your face with hors d'oeuvres, and partake heavily in the open bar if you so choose (but remember that too much may scare away that cutie or stud staring at you from across the dance floor).

It will likely take some time to find the right person (and you may have to kiss a lot of frogs), but throughout the process, you learn what you like and what you don't like. For example, as I briefly mentioned earlier, one short relationship from online dating many years ago taught me that even if a guy says he's romantic, it doesn't mean he necessarily is (empty adjective, anyone?), unless you call romantic being in bed at 10:00 every night without even making an exception for a casual game of Scrabble—my favorite. I was just so eager to be in a relationship at that time that I overlooked these things for a while. And I also had my fair share of awkward, yet laughable, experiences.

For the people I give "a little nudge" to, I don't let them quit after just one month of being online. It's not giving yourself a fair chance. Believe it or not, some people are still warming up to the whole concept of online dating, so maybe they just need time to get acclimated to the scene and to respond to you.

As Carrie once said on *Sex and the City*, "People go to casinos for the same reason they go on blind dates—hoping to hit the jackpot. But mostly, you just wind up broke or alone in a bar." Love is out there, but it just takes some good ol' time and some work to find it . . . and I'm here to help.

ABOUT THE AUTHOR

Erika Ettin grew up in Cherry Hill, NJ. She was actually a shy child until about seventh grade, when she decided to try her hand at acting. While she's certainly no Meryl Streep, she came out of her shell and is, to this day, perhaps the happiest, most animated person around.

Erika graduated from Cornell University in 2003 with a BA in economics and in 2009 from Georgetown University with an MBA. She worked in several financial roles at Fannie Mae in Washington, D.C. In March of 2011, she decided, after much introspection, that it was time to find greener pastures, in the form of quitting her job and starting her own business, A Little Nudge.

Erika built her business from the ground up, and she has worked with clients all around the United States and the world. She currently boasts client marriages/engagements in the double digits. Her work has been featured on NPR, *The Washington Post*, AskMen.com, WUSA9, CBS3, Fox29, *Roll Call*, *Business Insider*, and Refinery29.com. She also writes a weekly column for Philly.com, a monthly column for JDate, and has a syndicated column through the McClatchy-Tribune News Service. In addition, Erika has her own live radio show on Monday nights from 7:00 to 8:00 p.m. ET on www.listenvisionlife.com. Her dream is still to have her own TV show so she can share her passion for online dating and her tips for success with people around the world. Expect big things from Erika.

Erika currently lives in Washington, D.C., with her fabulous dog, Scruffy.

Given that this is a book sharing online dating advice, Erika thought she'd end her biography with a bit about herself in online dating profile form:

ABOUT ME

In some ways, I never grew out of my 11-year-old self: I love everything pink or sparkly (or both), I still think Disney World is the happiest place on earth, I often match my socks or shoes to my shirts, I love board games (especially Scrabble and Taboo), and I tend to laugh at my own jokes (mostly puns). But in other ways, I may have more in common with your grandma: I play a weekly game of mahjong, I make a killer brisket for all the holidays, and I carry a sweater around in every bag because I'm always cold.

But then again, I'm also a regular gal in her 30s who loves going to a good happy hour (I heart Scotch), singing in a karaoke league, and running my own business. I tend to march to the beat of my own drum, and not much embarrasses me, so I'll be the first one on the dance floor and the last one to leave a restaurant (indulging my foodie tendencies) if I'm enjoying myself.

Want more? www.alittlenudge.com

Twitter: @ALittleNudge

Email: info@alittlenudge.com

Phone: 202.71.NUDGE or 877.71.NUDGE

NOTES

Chapter 1

1. Adam Alter, "I See Red: The color you need to wear on your online dating profile," March 21, 2013, accessed July 12, 2014, http://slate.com/articles/double_x/doublex/2013/03/n ew_book_drunk_tank_pink_argues_red_is_the _color_for_dating_profiles.single.html

Chapter 12

2. Robert H. Thaler, Cass R. Sunstein, *Nudge: Improving Decisions About Health, Wealth, and Happiness* (London: Penguin Books, 2009), 113.

Chapter 15

3. Kris Ruby, "Millionaire Matchmaker Patti Stanger Teaches JDate Columnist Kris Ruby How to Get Married in a Year," January 2011, accessed May 28, 2014, http://www.jdate.com/jmag/2011/01 /millionaire-matchmaker-patti-stanger-how-to-get-married-in-a-year/

Chapter 17

4. Christian Rudder, "Online Dating Advice: Optimum Message Length," September 3, 2009, accessed May 28, 2014, http://blog.okcupid.com/index.php /how-to-get-people-to-reply-to-your-messages-in-online-dating-part-i/

Chapter 25

5. Laura Casey, "Attitudes about dating changing in this dour economy," *San Jose Mercury News*, July 26, 2011, accessed May 22, 2014, http://www.mercurynews.com/bay-area-living/ci_18546982?nclick_check=1

Chapter 27

6. "DTR," last modified March 9, 2003, http://www.urbandictionary.com/define .php?term=DTR

Chapter 28

7. Erin Scottberg, "The Top 10 Worst First Date No-Nos," May 5, 2013, accessed May 22, 2014, http://www.howaboutwe.com/date-report/ the-top-10-worst-first-date-no-nos/

Chapter 29

8. *Daily Mail* Reporter, "No text from a first date in 36 hours? Forget it, you've got no chance of a second," October 20, 2011, accessed May 22, 2014, http://www .dailymail.co.uk/news/article-2051178/No-text-date-36-hours-Forget-youve -got-chance-second.html

Chapter 30

9. "Dating," last modified August 17, 2003, http://www.urbandictionary.com /define.php?term=dating